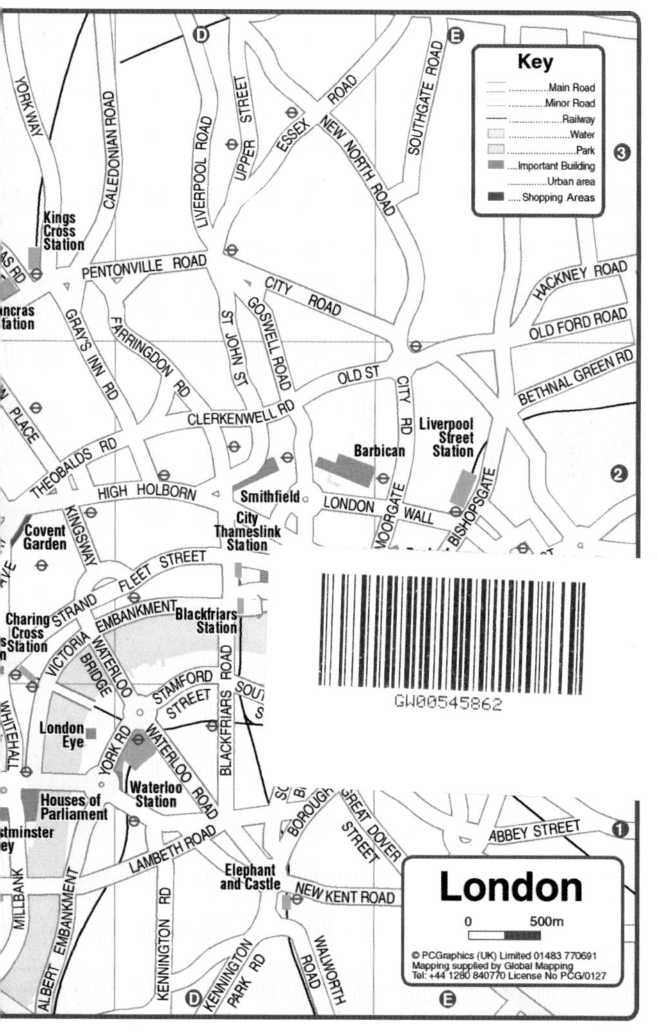

Key
Main Road
Minor Road
Railway
Water
Park
Important Building
Urban area
Shopping Areas
YORK WAY
CALEDONIAN ROAD
LIVERPOOL ROAD
UPPER STREET
ESSEX ROAD
NEW NORTH ROAD
SOUTHGATE ROAD
Kings Cross Station
PENTONVILLE ROAD
CITY ROAD
HACKNEY ROAD
OLD FORD ROAD
BETHNAL GREEN RD
GRAY'S INN RD
FARRINGDON RD
ST JOHN ST
GOSWELL ROAD
OLD ST
CITY RD
CLERKENWELL RD
THEOBALDS RD
HIGH HOLBORN
Liverpool Street Station
Barbican
Smithfield
LONDON WALL
MOORGATE
BISHOPSGATE
City Thameslink Station
Covent Garden
KINGSWAY
FLEET STREET
STRAND
EMBANKMENT
Blackfriars Station
Charing Cross Station
VICTORIA
WATERLOO BRIDGE
STAMFORD STREET
BLACKFRIARS ROAD
WHITEHALL
London Eye
YORK RD
WATERLOO ROAD
Waterloo Station
Houses of Parliament
BOROUGH
GREAT DOVER STREET
ABBEY STREET
LAMBETH ROAD
Elephant and Castle
NEW KENT ROAD
MILLBANK
ALBERT EMBANKMENT
KENNINGTON RD
KENNINGTON PARK RD
WALWORTH ROAD
London
0 500m
GW00545862

Memories of Ireland

A Digital View Of Ireland With A Song For Every County

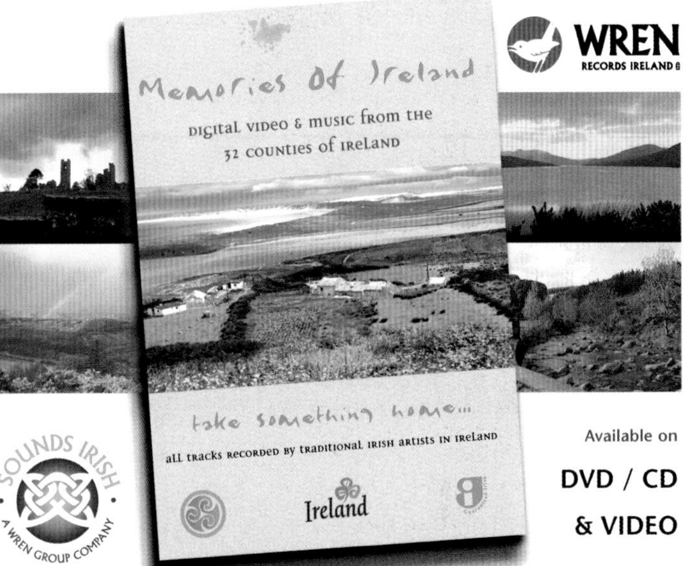

Available on

DVD / CD

& VIDEO

www.soundsirish.com

- One website for all your Irish Music needs
- A memory of all Counties
- A world wide playable DVD suitable for wide screen presentation

A website constantly updated with Irish music including Folk, Traditional, Ballads, Pub Songs

Free shipping on all orders

INSIDE THIS EDITION

Lloyd's Stock Exchange

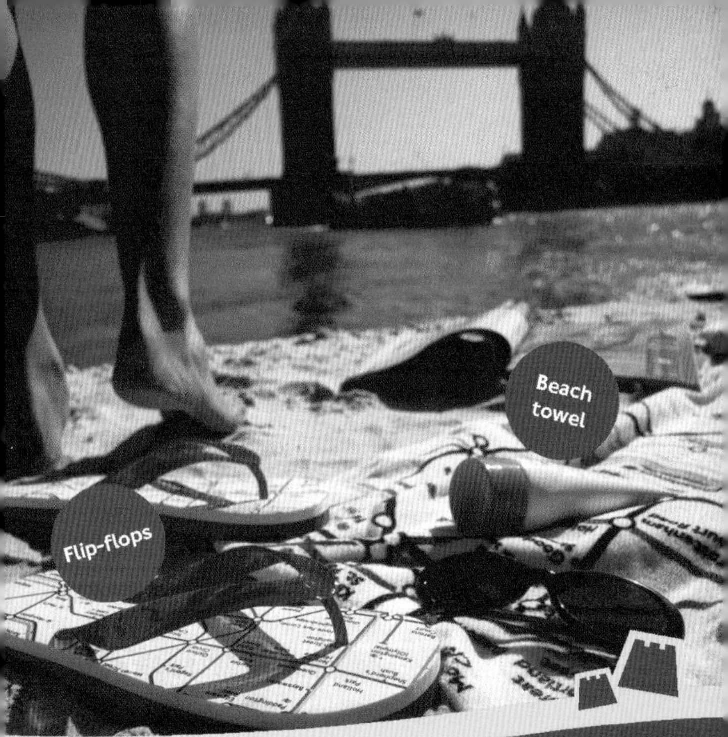

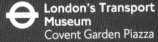

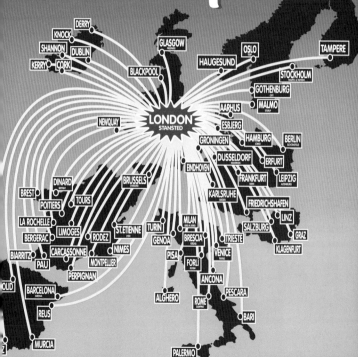

TRAVEL COMPANION

- Comprehensive guides to main attractions
- Excursions
- Nightlife & Entertainment
- Shopping Streets & Markets
- Greetings & Phrases in five languages
- Compact and factual guides for your weekend break or a longer stay

15 MINS FREE CALL CREDIT TO 19 COUNTRIES

London is a fascinating blend of heritage and tradition with dynamism and a talent for doing the unexpected. It's a mix which qualifies London as the first World City, where any of the planet's billions of people can feel at home. Whether you're looking for culture, shopping, dining, sightseeing or watching sport, London is a truly world-class destination for a day-trip, a weekend break or something longer.

The main influence in shaping the London of the twenty-first century has been the regular stream of immigrants over many centuries, giving Britain and its capital an unrivalled cultural diversity. The influences on language, music, cuisine, religion and every other aspect of life range from medieval Italian merchants to seventeenth-century French Huguenots and Jews fleeing pogroms in Eastern Europe in the nineteenth century. More recently in the 1950s, Britain's Caribbean and African colonies, and the newly independent countries of India, Pakistan and Sri Lanka, sent their people to work in the 'Mother Country'. At first, they worked menial jobs in hospitals, on the railways or driving buses, but gradually became important parts of a new, multi-racial, multi-cultural London.

By the start of the new millennium, the sight of a black or Asian government minister is unremarkable, Indian food is an integral part of the national diet, and Caribbean music and 'cool' are the style for second- and third-generation immigrants. Today, the typical cockney (Londoner) is as likely to have a Jamaican or Pakistani accent as he is to talk with an east London twang. And in recent years, the expansion of the EU and large influxes of war refugees have added even more to the fantastic racial mix that gives London its special feel – one first-grade school in the city reportedly gives lessons in forty-nine different languages.

Technically, London is two cities; London and Westminster, with numerous surrounding villages and towns (each with its own distinct character) merging into one giant metropolis. There are two mayors – the Lord Mayor, who heads local government in the City of London, and the Mayor of London, who runs the rest of the city – two fire brigades and two police forces, three if you include the transport police who patrol the Underground metro system. It's surprising that there's only one river!

w of London Eye from Westminster Bridge

The story of London cannot be separated from the River Thames. From Roman times onwards, the River Thames has been the central vein of life through the city. It was not by chance that medieval merchants established themselves on its banks, to where ships brought exotic spices and wines from the Mediterranean and the East, and took English wool to Northern Europe. Now, although the docklands of the Port of London have been redeveloped for housing and commerce, the river serves as a constant reminder of the former power of

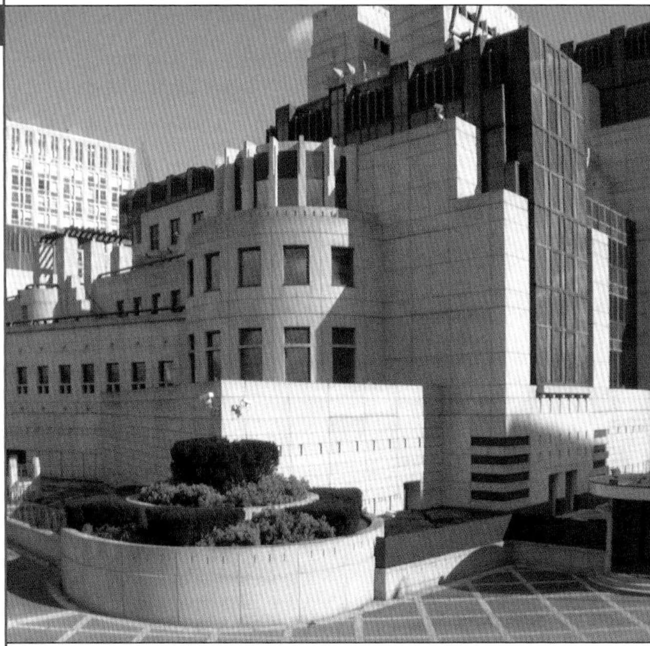

MI5, an example of London's eclectic architecture

London as a major seaport and, for 200 years, the main trading centre for the largest empire the world has known.

After the end of the Second World War, London was a city which, if not actually in decline, was going nowhere fast. Whole communities were moved out of areas flattened in the Blitz and transplanted to rural towns such as St Neots, Cambridgeshire, or to 'new towns' such as Bracknell and Stevenage. The central part of the city was deserted by most of its residents. Those Londoners who remained were housed in the ugly tower apartment blocks which typified 1960s architecture. The population of Greater London fell drastically from 10 million at its peak to its current number of 7.5 million.

Eros, [P]illy Circus, a common [me]eting place for tourists

Things started changing for the better in the 1970s. The economic boom of the 1980s transformed not only the commercial centre ('the City') but also the whole of London. Money was suddenly readily available and London knew how to spend it on cutting-edge architecture and furniture, haute cuisine restaurants, champagne in dance clubs and fast cars. Conspicuous consumption and excess were symbolic of the eighties and early nineties, even when the economic boom later turned temporarily to bust.

World-class architects such as Sir Richard Rogers, Sir James Stirling, Argentine César Pelli and the Swiss team of Herzog and de Meuron have transformed the

A view through Tower Bridge

physical look of the city in just two short decades. The concrete block approach epitomised by Sir Denys Lasdun's National Theatre complex has been replaced by experimentation, new materials, a sense of humour and the matching of buildings to the people who will use them, not the other way around. Even those with only a passing interest in architecture cannot but be impressed by the originality, exuberance and often sheer beauty of London's new buildings. These include the Swiss Re building, Lloyd's of London, Canada Tower at Canary Wharf, Charing Cross Station and their precursor, the Telecom Tower (still called the Post Office Tower by many) which dates from 1964.

Today, the new London is cleaner than it was twenty years ago, the people are friendlier and there is a buzz of prosperity which even the most jaded visitor will enjoy. Dr Johnson's opinion of London is as true now as when he said in 1777: 'When a man is tired of London, he is tired of life, for there is in London all that life can afford'.

Currency and Banking

The currency in the United Kingdom is the pound sterling (£), which is divided into 100 pence (p). Notes come in £50, £20, £10 and £5 denominations, while coins in circulation are £2, £1, 50p, 20p, 10p, 5p, 2p and 1p. Notes are issued by the **Bank of England** but you may see some issued by Scottish or Northern Irish banks. Although some shops may accept them, they are not legal tender in England and Wales and you should ask for English notes instead. Many businesses, especially larger shops and even some supermarkets, will also accept the Euro and the US dollar.

Bank of England, Threadneedle Street

Banking hours are 9.30am to 3.30pm but many stay open later than this. Cash machines (ATMs) are available everywhere. Many Londoners rarely visit their bank branch but use ATMs and Internet banking instead. Currency can be exchanged at a range of banks, building societies, post offices and **bureaux de change**. Banks usually give the best exchange rates, although bureaux de change tend to stay open later. International credit cards can be used in most places.

Competition among shops, pubs and restaurants is fierce. You'll often get a better price if you are prepared to look around.

Bank Station Underground

Expect to pay more in pubs and restaurants in the West End and the City. Tips in restaurants and taxis are usually 10% but check a service charge hasn't already been added to your bill. Do not tip bar staff in pubs or try to run a tab; neither is part of British pub culture.

Transport

London has one of the best public transport networks of any city, combining the **Underground**, urban railways, buses and thousands of taxis. The system has been neglected in recent years, but new investment and better planning are already showing improvements. Ticketing is now integrated, which means you can buy a daily or weekly **Travelcard** which will let you use any combination of tube, rail and bus.

The best way of travelling from the airport is by train or on the Underground (tube). From **Heathrow**, the Underground will take you to the city centre in about

The classic Routemaster double-decker bus

forty-five minutes, or you can pay slightly more on the train and get to **Paddington Station** in fifteen. The last trains are at midnight. The **Gatwick Express** runs from the airport to **Victoria Station** from 5.20am to 1.35am with four trains every hour. The **Stansted Express** takes forty-five minutes from the airport to **Liverpool Street Station.** Coach services run from each airport to **Victoria Coach Station**. Coaches are cheaper than the train, but take longer.

The Underground (also known as 'the tube') is the easiest way to get around, but avoid headaches and confusion by not travelling at rush hour (8.00am - 9.30am and 4.30pm - 6.30pm) when trains are very crowded. There is a network of twelve lines criss-crossing central and Greater London. Each line is marked in a different colour on the route map which looks confusing at first but is easy to understand with practice. Tickets are priced according to a series of zones and there are a wide variety of discounted fares. The cheapest journey in Zone 1 (the West End and the City) is £2. Long queues at the ticket office are now a thing of the past thanks to the automatic machines which are at every station.

London has fourteen railway stations, each of which has a nearby Underground station. Most rail passengers are commuters from the outer suburbs or even further afield. Visitors are most likely to use one of the eight main line stations when they are travelling out of London on a day trip or to another part of Britain. There is also the **Docklands Light Railway**, which links the city centre with the old London docks. The docks are now a modern commercial and financial centre dominated by Canary Wharf, a fifty-storey development which is the tallest office block in Europe.

The red double-decker **London bus** is an iconic image recognised around the world. There are still a few of the traditional Routemaster buses operating, complete with an open entry platform at the rear and a conductor who collects your fare. For the more modern buses with a central entry door, you have to buy a ticket in advance from a machine at the bus stop. You can also buy discount bus passes at newsagents and Underground stations. Like the Underground, fares are charged according to the zone you travel in; a journey in the central zone is £1. Routes are identified by numbers and maps showing every bus route and the main destinations are displayed

Liverpool Street Railway Station

Black cab; all are fitted with wheelchair ramps

at bus stops and Underground stations. Buses are a great way to see the sights of London but traffic congestion can make journeys longer than if you went by tube.

The traditional London **black cab** (taxi) is fast becoming a thing of the past, with many now painted in a range of blues, greens and greys, often with advertising splashed on the sides or bonnet. The typical London cabby (driver) remains one of the city's greatest characters. Ask for his opinion on anything from George Bush to Real Madrid or where to find a good Indian restaurant and you'll get an entertaining monologue in reply. Fares are relatively expensive compared with continental European cities – a short ten-minute journey might cost £5 or more – but the five-seater cabs are a quick way of getting around in comfort. There are cab ranks all over the city but the easiest way to get one is to wave the driver down on the street. If the roof light is yellow, the cab is free for hire.

Most people visiting London see the sites while walking or using public transport. However, if you want to hire a car to visit somewhere further afield, such as Oxford or Cambridge, you will need a valid driving licence and a credit card. If you are renting a car, we recommend **Hertz**, located at each airport and at various offices in the city. Driving in central London can be time-consuming and you will have to pay a £5 daily congestion charge to enter certain areas between 7.00am and 6.30pm. The charge was introduced by Ken

London tour bus

Livingstone, the radical and charismatic Mayor of London, against the government's wishes, but it seems to be succeeding in reducing the amount of traffic in the city centre. This, in turn, means that pedestrians are safer crossing roads and there is less exhaust pollution. The area covered by the charge is roughly the West End, the City and a small corner of the south bank around Waterloo and Southwalk. Electronic sensors on the roadside check whether you have a valid sticker and penalties for not having one are high; fines of up to £125 and clamping of your vehicle.

Tours

The best way for the first-time visitor, or even the veteran, to see London is from the top of one of the open-topped double-decker buses which operate daily. The **Original Tour** and **Big Bus** companies have hop-on, hop-off services on various routes taking in the main historic and cultural sights. You can start and finish, or simply take a break, anywhere along your route. Bus stops are well sign-posted and tickets can be bought on the bus or in advance through your hotel or any **Tourist Information Centre**.

Cruise boat operators run services along the length of the River Thames from Hampton Court to the Thames Barrier. The boats give you a completely different view of the Palace of Westminster or the Tower of London and can be picked up at numerous jetties and piers on both banks.

More energetic visitors can go on one of the many guided walking tours on offer with themes ranging from ghosts, Jack the Ripper, the London of Charles Dickens to famous buildings and even plain old pub crawls. Most tours start at a tube station. It's worth checking if your guide has a Blue Badge qualification from the **London Tourist Board** to be guaranteed expert knowledge and value for money. Don't hand over cash to anyone until you know for certain that they are your guide – conmen have been known to target visitors.

Golden gates to Green Park

Westminster has been the seat of political and religious power in England for one thousand years, and **Whitehall** has been the home of the politicians and civil servants who have presided over Britain's chequered history. It is here that English kings and queens have been crowned since 1066 and, in 1649, where **King Charles I** was beheaded. Today, commercial power in London is centred on the City, but government authority comes from Westminster and Whitehall.

If you stand on **Westminster Bridge** and look west, you will see the most famous view in Britain, the **Palace of Westminster** and its stately clock tower, known to most people as **Big Ben** (although Ben is actually the giant bell inside which rings on the hour and quarter-hour). There has been a royal palace on this site for nearly one thousand years; the oldest part, **Westminster Hall,** dates from 1097. But, since 1512, the palace has been the meeting place for the two houses of parliament; the **Commons**, who are elected, and the **Lords**, who are appointed. Visitors can view the fine wood panelling, the frescoes and busts of political leaders in the corridors and galleries of the palace, but most people go to see **Members of Parliament** (MPs) debating the issues of the day. Security at Westminster is tight and places in the public gallery are limited, so expect to queue.

Westminster Abbey

On the opposite side of St Margaret's Street is **Westminster Abbey,** the most obvious symbol of the role religion has

Palace of Westminster and Big Ben

played historically in affairs of state. This is where England's kings and queens are crowned and most monarchs up to the mid-eighteenth century are buried here. The tomb of **Elizabeth I** is particularly impressive. The abbey was founded in 1065 and was largely completed in Gothic style by 1400. The building was added to over succeeding centuries; the famous neo-Gothic West Towers at the entrance to the abbey were only completed in 1745 to a design by **Nicholas Hawksmoor**, a former pupil of **Sir Christopher Wren**. Inside, the interest for most visitors is more historical and cultural than religious. **Poets' Corner** is devoted to the memory of famous writers such as **Chaucer, Shakespeare** and **Dickens**. Buried among the kings and queens is the **Unknown Warrior**, an unidentified soldier who died in the **First World War** and whose tomb commemorates all those who lost their lives.

The abbey dwarfs **St Margaret's Church**, the parish church of the **House of Commons**. This restored fifteenth-century church still retains some Tudor features, including a Flemish stained glass window presented by Ferdinand and Isabella of Spain on the engagement of **Catherine of Aragon** to **Prince Arthur**. Arthur died before the window arrived and his brother, **Henry VIII**, married Catherine. Later, when Henry was denied a divorce by the Pope, he split with Rome and established the protestant **Church of England**, one of the most important events in the history of both Britain and Europe. He went on to have another five wives and the window was kept hidden away at **Waltham Abbey** until it was finally sent to St Margaret's more than 200 years later.

Impressive though it is, **Westminster Abbey**, like St Paul's Cathedral in the City, often struggles to balance the demands of sightseers' with its religious role. The abbey is often crowded and noisy during the tourist season and the range of admission charges for different chapels can make the abbey seem more like a tourist attraction than a religious institution.

Past **New Scotland Yard**, home of the **Metropolitan Police**, is an all-together more serene place of worship, **Westminster Cathedral**, the most important Roman Catholic cathedral in Britain. Completed in Italian-Byzantine style in 1903, the red and white brick exterior contrasts with the mosaics and marbles inside. The acoustics are haunting and there are few sounds more uplifting than the daily sung Mass (Mon-Fri 5.30pm, Sat, Sun 10.30am).

North of **Parliament Square**, the first roundabout in Britain (1926), and the **Houses of Parliament** is an area known as Whitehall. Whitehall itself is a street which follows on from Parliament Street, but its name is now synonymous with central government and the civil

Victoria Tower Gardens and Houses of Parliament

service. **Dover House**, an impressive Georgian mansion built in 1787, now houses the **Scottish Office. The Banqueting House**, designed in Classic Palladian style by **Inigo Jones** in 1622, features ceiling paintings by **Rubens. Charles I** was beheaded on a scaffold erected in the courtyard outside it. **Horse Guards**, an elegant building with an impressive clock tower, dates from 1753. Mounted soldiers of the **Household Cavalry** provide a guard here which is ceremonially changed every day. Behind Horse Guards is a large parade ground which was once Henry VIII's tournament ground, but is now better known for the colourful annual military ceremony of **Trooping the Colour**.

The most famous location in the area is **Downing Street**, which is closed to the public for security reasons. However, you can look through the iron security gates from the pavement in Whitehall and still see **No 10**, where every British **Prime Minister** since 1732 has lived. **The Cabinet War Rooms**, where **Winston Churchill** and his colleagues ran the Allied effort during the **Second World War**, are worth visiting. The government was able to continue functioning here, protected by reinforced concrete, even as German bombs fell on London during the **Blitz** (1940-41). The jumble of underground rooms have been laid out as

Horse Guards parade

they were in 1945, when the war ended. Churchill famously did much of his work in bed, which is preserved along with his desk.

Whitehall's towering grandeur makes the annual **Remembrance Day** ceremony, commemorating the dead, all the more solemn and impressive. Wreaths of poppies are laid at the **Cenotaph** by the Queen, other dignitaries and ordinary people who gravely parade past. Nearby, at the corner by **Westminster Bridge**, is a stirring statue of **Boudicca**, the British queen who rose against the Romans in 61 AD and sacked London before the rebellion was quashed.

Admiralty Arch, a giant triple archway designed by **Aston Webb** in 1911, has government offices and even 'grace and favour' apartments for ministers in its structure. While ordinary traffic can pass through the two side arches, the middle is reserved for royal

Cenotaph Memorial Monument

carriages on State occasions. Walking through to the other side of the arch shows why: The Mall stretches ahead for nearly 1km, giving an uninterrupted view of Buckingham Palace, the official home of the British monarch.

The Mall runs along the north side of **St James's Park**, London's oldest park and a popular place for a stroll at any time of the day or year. Cows still grazed on what was drained marshland when **John Nash** landscaped the park in 1829. Nash included a lake with islands which are now home to ducks, black swans and even pelicans. When you get to the **Queen Victoria Memorial** at the bottom of The Mall you are in the middle of what is best described as a royal ghetto, with five royal palaces in a row. **Marlborough House**, home of the nineteenth-century **Prince of Wales**, is now the headquarters of the Commonwealth Secretariat. **St James's Palace** was the Royal Family's official London residence for 140 years until **Queen Victoria** came to the throne; foreign diplomats are still officially accredited to 'the Court of St James's'.

Nowadays, senior courtiers and royal pensioners, not to mention the odd prince and princess, occupy the many apartments in the palace. **Clarence House** is now the

The Mall, the elegant avenue and ceremonial route to Buckingham Palace

London home of the current Prince of Wales, **Prince Charles**, and was designed by Nash for **William IV** in 1827. The **Queen Mother** lived in Clarence House for half a century until her death, aged 103, in 2003. **Lancaster House** was begun in 1825 for the **Duke of York** and was for many years home to the **London Museum**. Recently, it has been used as a government conference centre. The agreement giving full independence to Zimbabwe was negotiated here.

In 1837, the newly-crowned Queen Victoria moved into **Buckingham Palace** and it has been the headquarters for the reigning monarch ever since. The neo-classical east front facing The Mall was added in 1913. When the sovereign is in residence, the royal standard flies over the palace day and night and soldiers of the **Guards Division** in full uniform provide the guard. Tourists of all ages are always trying to get the soldiers to laugh as they stand rigidly to attention in their sentry boxes, dressed in heavy red tunics and tall bearskin hats (known as a busby). To their credit, the guardsmen rarely flinch or allow a flicker of a smile. **The Changing of the Guard**, a colourful ceremony performed to the

Plaque dedicated to Diana, Princess of Wales in St James's Park

Buckingham Palace, residence of the British monarch

music of a military band (11.30am daily April to August and every second day otherwise) is well worth seeing. At the same time, the Household Cavalry rides past Buckingham Palace to change the guard at **Horse Guards**.

The area in front of the gates of the palace is a traditional gathering place in times of national celebration, such as a royal wedding, a jubilee, or even the winning of a war. In 1945, **George VI** broke with precedent and asked Churchill, the victorious war leader and a commoner, to join him and the queen on the balcony to accept the cheers of the crowd below. **The State Rooms**, where guests are wined and dined at formal dinners and balls, are open to the public in summer in order to raise money to fund the restoration of Windsor Castle. You can buy your ticket from the booth at the bottom of The Mall.

The **Queen's Gallery** in **Buckingham Palace Gate** houses one of the most valuable private art collections in the world. It was built up over centuries by different monarchs and now includes works by **Canaletto, da**

Vinci and **Vermeer**, among other great masters. There are also exhibitions of jewels, porcelain, furniture and manuscripts. Nearby are the **Royal Mews**, where state coaches and carriages used by monarchs over the years are displayed: the spectacular Golden State Coach built for **George III** in 1761 is still used at coronations; the Irish State Coach is used every year at the state opening of parliament; and the Glass Coach is paraded at royal weddings. A number of official cars, including fabulous Rolls Royce Phantom Vs, Bentleys and Jaguars are also on display.

Shakespeare's Globe Theatre and Tate Modern

South of the **Houses of Parliament**, on Millbank on the north bank of the Thames between Lambeth Bridge and Vauxhall Bridge, is **Tate Britain**. Formerly known as the Tate Gallery, Tate Britain has the world's largest collection of British art from the sixteenth century to the present. Artists represented include: Constable, Whistler, Turner, Reynolds, Stubbs, Blake (William and Peter), Hockney, Lucian Freud, Francis Bacon and Damien Hirst. **The Clore Gallery**, a modernist design by **Sir James Stirling** attached to the main gallery, houses the **Turner Bequest**, left to the nation by the great landscape artist in 1851. The balance of the Tate Britain collection, twentieth- and twenty-first century modern art, is now housed in the Tate Modern.

Griffin Statue

The City has been the financial centre of London since medieval times and occupies a part of the north bank of the Thames originally settled by the Romans. Parts of the city wall built by the Romans after Boudicca's rebellion can still be seen. The most impressive section, 10m high, is at **Tower Hill** Underground station.

At **Charing Cross Station**, walk downstream on the **Victoria Embankment**, the vast stone banking for the **River Thames** which replaced the rotting wooden wharves of old London. While building the embankment, the Victorians also completed **Victoria Embankment Gardens**, a small but beautifully maintained public park famous for its musical concerts in the summer. Opposite the gates to the gardens stands **Cleopatra's needle**, a pink granite obelisk dating from 1500 BC and guarded by two bronze sphinxes. It was brought to Britain from Egypt in 1819 and has a twin in

Sphinx on the banks of the Thames

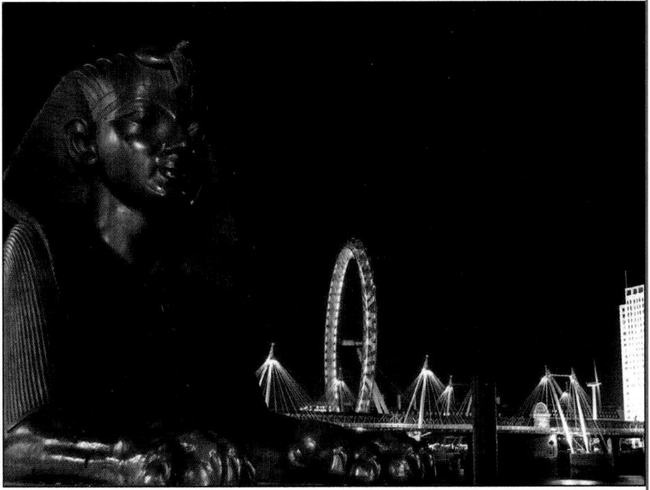

HMS Belfast

New York. Further downstream is the majestic **Somerset House**, now home to the **Courtauld Institute**. Its world famous collection of Impressionist paintings include works by **Degas**, **Manet** and **Van Gogh**.

The bridges and ships of the Thames make a stirring sight from the **Embankment**. Ships moored on the many piers and jetties on both banks range from river launches for hire and decommissioned Royal Navy warships such as ***HMS Chrysanthemum*** and ***HMS Belfast*** to the ***Golden Hinde***, a working replica of the fifteenth-century ship in which **Sir Francis Drake** circumnavigated the world.

Lancaster Place leads you by the side of Somerset House to **the Strand**. At the east end of the Strand are the **Royal Courts of Justice**, the main law courts in Britain, where the pavement is often blocked by television crews filming reports on important or sensational cases. On the other side of the road are

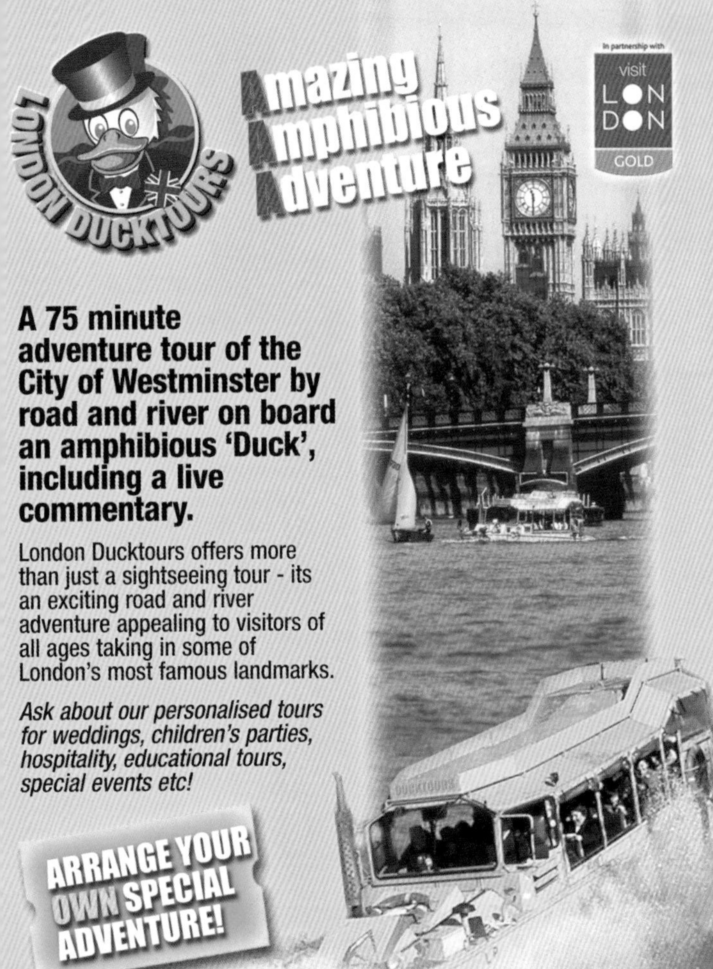
LONDON DUCKTOURS
Amazing
Amphibious
Adventure
in partnership with
visit
LONDON
GOLD
A 75 minute adventure tour of the City of Westminster by road and river on board an amphibious 'Duck', including a live commentary.
London Ducktours offers more than just a sightseeing tour - its an exciting road and river adventure appealing to visitors of all ages taking in some of London's most famous landmarks.
Ask about our personalised tours for weddings, children's parties, hospitality, educational tours, special events etc!
ARRANGE YOUR OWN SPECIAL ADVENTURE!
DUCKTOURS
www.londonducktours.co.uk 020 7928 3132

Ruins of old London

The Temple and **Middle Temple Hall** which still serve as working chambers for groups of lawyers. **The Old Bailey,** with its famous golden rooftop statue of the figure of Justice, is the main criminal court and is just north of Ludgate Circus, on the site of the notorious **Newgate prison**.

Fleet Street is a continuation of the Strand, so named because of the River Fleet, a small tributary of the Thames that flows beneath. Fleet Street is the commonly-used collective name given to Britain's national newspapers but the journalists and the printing presses have since moved down river to the redeveloped **Wapping** and **Docklands**. Many are now located in the giant **Canary Wharf** office complex.

St Paul's Cathedral and the Millennium Bridge

St Paul's Cathedral

St Bride's Church, set back from Fleet Street, has long-standing links with the written word. The first printing press with moveable type was operated in the church from 1500 and **Samuel Pepys**, the famous diarist, was christened here. The remains of a Roman walkway can be seen in the crypt.

Walk up the shallow incline of **Ludgate Hill** and you are faced with the front of **St Paul's Cathedral**, Sir Christopher Wren's greatest achievement and one of the symbols of British defiance during the dark days of the Blitz. After the disastrous **Great Fire** of 1666 – which destroyed 13,000 houses and scores of public buildings and churches, including the old wooden medieval cathedral – Wren was commissioned by **Charles II** to rebuild London as a modern seventeenth-century capital city using stone rather than flammable wood. Wren rebuilt fifty-two other churches but none is more impressive than St Paul's.

The interior is a Baroque masterpiece, with frescoes, wrought ironwork and towering columns. The great dome is 110m high, second in the world only to St Peter's in Rome. The unusual acoustics inside give rise to the name of the **Whispering Gallery**, where even the softest whisper can be clearly heard from the other side. North of St Paul's in Clerkenwell, you'll find the

The Gerkin building behind the Tower of London

Museum of the Order of St John at St John's Gate, where you can discover the rich history of the crusading Knights Hospitaller.

On **Queen Victoria Street** to the south of the cathedral is the **Mansion House**, a Georgian building which is the official residence of the **Lord Mayor of London.** On your left are the windowless walls and austere front of the **Bank of England**, from where the nation's currency has been managed for centuries, and where there is a museum, complete with real gold bars on display.

This area of the City is a curious mix of uninspiring old Victorian buildings, Georgian masterpieces and modern office blocks, often of the merely functional variety. Truly outstanding modern design is typified by three offices in the area. Where Queen Victoria Street meets a street with the unusual name of Poultry, is **No 1 Poultry**, unveiled in 1997. Designed by Sir James

Stirling, it is an eye-catching mélange of angles, arcs, circles and balconies in reddish sand and grey concrete. In the distance you can see the high-tech **Swiss Re building**. Shaped like a giant artillery shell, forty-one storeys high, and nicknamed **'the Gerkin'**, it claims to be the first ecological sky-scraper in London, using ambient air from outside to control the environment within the building. Better known is the spectacular **Lloyds of London** building on nearby **Lime Street**, completed by **Sir Richard Rogers** in 1986. If the external piping and high-tech ducts look familiar, that's because Rogers also designed the similar-looking, but smaller, Pompidou Centre in Paris.

On **Aldgate**, turn south onto the **Minories** and you are on the edge of **Whitechapel**, where **Jack the Ripper** savagely murdered six women in 1888. The slums and tenements of what was once the poorest part of London are now gone, replaced by new public housing and commercial office blocks. You can get a flavour of the terror Jack brought to the **East End** on a walking tour with **Gren Tours** which will bring you to the six murder sites, review the evidence and talk about the suspects. Glen Tours also offers walking tours of Royal London and Rock 'n' Roll London, as well as chauffeur tours of the city and beyond.

At the bottom of the Minories is Tower Hill and the imposing **Tower of London**. There has been a castle on the site since 1078, when **William the Conqueror** strengthened his grip on England's capital city. In the past 900 years it has served as a potent symbol of political and military might, a royal palace, a prison, an armoury, the royal mint, the royal treasury and a private royal zoo. Important prisoners in the past include **James I** of Scotland, **John the Good** of France, **Princess Elizabeth** (later Queen Elizabeth I), **Sir Walter Raleigh** and **Rudolph Hess**, the Nazi leader. Those executed here by order of the monarch include **Sir Thomas More**, two of Henry VIII's queens (at his own command), the **Duke of Monmouth** and a number of German spies during the Second World War.

The London Dungeon Exhibition

Parts of the Tower were first opened to the public by **Charles II** in the late-1600s and it is now London's number one attraction. It is easy to see why; visitors can view the priceless **Crown Jewels**, including the crown worn by a monarch during the coronation ceremony, displays of historic weapons and armour, including Henry VIII's suit of armour, and other valuable royal artefacts.

Alongside it is **Tower Bridge** (1894), one of the enduring symbols of London, although visitors often wrongly call it **London Bridge**, which is further upstream. With its twin towers and linking catwalk, it is a masterpiece of Victorian engineering and still lifts its central bridge daily to allow ships up-river. The **Tower Bridge Exhibition** has interactive displays of the bridge's history and you can visit the original steam engines which powered the lifting machinery. Between London Bridge and Tower bridge, you will find **Winston Churchill's Britain at War Experience** on Tooley Street where you can walk through London during the Blitz and experience what life was like during WWII.

If you walk back along the **Thames Path** towards Westminster, before London Bridge is **The Monument**. The tallest isolated stone column in the world (62m), it was designed by Wren to commemorate the Great Fire and stands 62m away from the pie shop in **Pudding Lane** where the fire started. Views from the top are spectacular.

The inner arc of the Thames either side of **Waterloo Bridge** is a cultural wonderland, with theatres, concert halls and galleries aplenty. At night, the south bank is alive with audiences coming and going from the various venues. East of the bridge, a favourite place

Statue of Boudicca with London Eye in the background

for London's more talented buskers, is the **Royal National Theatre**, a complex which has three separate theatres with a total of 2,400 seats, as well as a 1,000-seater restaurant. The modernist concrete structure by Sir Denys Lasdun was much criticised when it opened in 1976, but is now a familiar part of the South Bank.

Downstream, past the **OXO Tower**, built in 1928 to advertise the popular meat cooking stock, is **Tate Modern**, where the Tate Gallery's collection of twentieth and twenty-first century modern art is now housed in the imaginatively converted old **Bankside Power Station.**

Shakespeare's **Globe Theatre**, the pet project of American film director **Sam Wannamaker**, where Shakespeare's plays were first performed, is popular architecturally and historically. Like the original, the Globe is round and only partly roofed, and audiences are encouraged to get involved in the plays. Most performances are in the summer, for obvious reasons. Close by is the **Millennium footbridge**, which spans the river.

West of Waterloo Bridge are the **National Film Theatre** and the **Hayward Gallery**, a stark grey concrete relic of 'Brutalist' 1960s architecture which specialises in the works of contemporary artists. Nearby is the **South Bank Centre**, a venue for live music made up of three concert halls. Past **Jubilee Gardens** is the British Airways **London Eye**, a ferris wheel which dominates the skyline on both banks of the river. Buy your ticket early in the day or be prepared for long queues to see the spectacular views across the city. Just behind here, on Chicheley Street, you can catch one of **London Ducktours'** amphibious buses which drive past London's famous landmarks before launching into the River Thames at Vauxhall.

The Imperial War Museum on **Lambeth Road** covers the history of two world wars and occupies the old **Bethlem Royal Hospital**, the lunatic asylum which gave its name to the word 'bedlam'. Exhibits include aircraft, tanks and artillery from both wars, including **Field Marshall Montgomery**'s command tank. Nearby is **Lambeth Palace**, the London base of the **Archbishop of Canterbury**, the spiritual head of the Church of England.

The Millennium Dome

Queen Elizabeth Gate to Hyde Park

These days, the 'West End' is neither in the west nor at the end of London. But, when the name was coined, it was a prosperous, newly-developed area situated to the west of the old city of London. Traditionally associated with luxury shopping and theatres, the West End is the beating heart of London.

Hyde Park Corner, where Constitution Hill, Knightsbridge, Park Lane and Piccadilly meet, is the busiest road junction in London. In the middle of all this is the **Wellington Arch**, commemorating Wellington's victory at Waterloo. The Iron Duke's links to the area are strong. He lived in **Apsley House**, which faces the arch, and socialised in **Pall Mall** and **Piccadilly**. Look out for the interesting tile murals telling his life story in the Hyde Park Corner underpass.

A stroll up Piccadilly, which is bordered to the south by **Green Park**, takes you past London's tribute to the late Princess of Wales. Opposite the junction with Half Moon Street are memorial gates to **Princess Diana** and the starting point for the **Diana, Princess of Wales Memorial Walk** in Green Park. **Langan's Brasserie** on Stratton Street, to the left off Piccadilly, was one of the first of the new wave of innovative restaurants when it opened in the 1970s; it still has a fin-de-siècle feel but the celeb diners are long gone. As you walk from **Berkeley Street** to Berkeley Square you'll find yourself in the heart of swanky **Mayfair**. It remains one of London's prettiest squares, although the environment of modern London means the nightingale may no longer sing there, as the old song claimed.

The **Burlington Arcade** (1819) was originally designed to house an arcade of shops selling luxury goods, and it still does today. The **Royal Academy of Arts** next door is an all-together different building, one of the few remaining Georgian West End mansions. The courtyard has a series of small fountains which cascade over the central paving. There are permanent displays but the academy is most famous for its summer art exhibition, which has been held annually for over 200 years.

Across the road is the **Ritz Hotel,** founded by César Ritz in 1906, and it's still as stylishly gaudy as its name implies. **Fortnum and Mason**, the

Trafalgar Square

department store famous for its food delicacies, is close by. At the end of Piccadilly is **Piccadilly Circus**, where the statue of **Eros**, the Greek god of love, has presided since 1892 and should by now be accustomed to the huge flashing neon advertisements, which serve to light up the sides of the buildings surrounding the circus at night.

Trafalgar Square (1830s), to the southeast of Piccadilly Circus down Haymarket, has played host to many demonstrations and New Year's Eve celebrations over the decades. The square is dominated by the 50m-high Nelson's Column, which commemorates Britain's most famous naval hero. Four statues depicting lions by **Sir Edwin Landseer** guard its base. On the north side of the square is the **National Gallery**, a monumental Neo-Classical building which houses one of the world's greatest art collections. Highlights among the thousands of exhibits from the early Renaissance onwards include cartoons by **da Vinci**, **Hans Holbein**'s painting *The Ambassadors*, and **Van Gogh**'s *Sunflowers*. The **National Portrait Gallery** is home to a fantastic collection of portraits of some of Britain's cultural, political and sporting icons and is well worth a visit. To the northeast of the square is the church of **St Martin-in-the-Fields**, rebuilt in 1726 by **James Gibbs** and famous the world over for its choir and concerts. There is a small arts and crafts market open daily in the grounds.

To the north is **Leicester Square**, which has been a centre of entertainment for centuries, whether it has been Restoration theatre, Victorian music hall or twentieth-century cinema. So it is fitting that the small garden known as Leicester Fields has statues of **Shakespeare** and **Charlie Chaplin**, both famous Londoners.

East of Leicester Square is **Covent Garden**, once the city's main fruit and vegetable market but now housing crafts shops, books, designer clothing and antiques. Covent Garden also provides its guests with live

Chinatown in Soho

entertainment, a feature for centuries and a tradition that continues today, where an array of musicians, jugglers, fire-eaters and other street entertainers perform for the amused crowd.

When you follow Shaftesbury Avenue westwards to Piccadilly Circus you'll meet the start of **Regent Street**, one of the capital's finest shopping areas. The graceful curve of terraced stone shopfronts is one of the great sights in London. In between Regent Street and Charing Cross Road, itself famous for its bookstores, is **Soho**, an area of London whose very name was synonymous with sleaze. Today, Soho is more than just a few strip clubs and massage parlours. Chinese immigrants have created a small **Chinatown** around Gerrard Street, and the regulars at the **Coach and Horses** pub on Greek Street are as eclectic as ever.

To the northeast of Soho is the **British Museum**, one of London's leading tourist attractions. The museum has one of the greatest collections of art and antiquities from the ancient world. The stars of the show are artefacts from the **Sutton Hoo Treasure**: jewellery, coins, weapons and a stunning gold ceremonial helmet, all of which were found in the grave of a seventh-century Anglo-Saxon king in Sutton Hoo, Suffolk. The **British Library** on Euston Road has a fine display of manuscripts that include two of the original four copies of **Magna Carta** (1215), one of the main documents of the British constitution, the **Lindisfarne Gospels**, religious tracts dating back to the eighth century, and the original lyric sheet of the **Beatles** song *Yesterday*.

North of **Oxford Street** are **Regent's Park** and **London Zoo**. The park is a former royal hunting ground and has an open-air theatre where performances of Shakespeare take place in the summer. Its landscaped gardens include a boating lake and a children's playground. London Zoo was founded in 1826 and attracts more than two million visitors a year. Its primates and Giant Pandas prove to be the greatest attractions. It is also a leading zoological research centre.

At the western end of Oxford Street is **Marble Arch**, which recently underwent cleaning and restoration. It stands close to **Tyburn**, the gory site of London's executions for over 600 years. More than 60,000 people died here up to 1793 and a plaque set in the pavement marks the exact location of the gallows.

Hyde Park, opened to the public in 1635, has had a lively history, serving as a military depot in two world

Speakers' Corner, Hyde Park

wars, the site of the **1851 Great Exhibition**, the venue for the **1984 Live Aid** concert and the focal point for many political demonstrations over the years. It is the largest open space in London and you can enjoy its long walks, or maybe hire paddle boats to cruise its **Serpentine Lake**. The bandstand is still used on summer Sundays, as are the football pitches and 8km of bridle paths. Horses can be hired from local stables. In times past, society people paraded on horseback on **Rotten Row**, a straight 2km track along the south side. Every Sunday afternoon, **Speakers' Corner**, near Marble Arch, resounds to the noise of open air debates on any subject; political, religious, or just plain silly, this always attract large crowds. Anyone can stand up and speak but be prepared to answer merciless barracking from the 'professional' hecklers (they have their own club).

Natural History Museum

Down **Kensington Road**, which runs along the south side of the park, is the **Royal Albert Hall**, flanked by the **Royal College of Art** and the **Royal Geographical Society**. Opened in 1870 as a memorial to Queen Victoria's late husband, this glass-domed building is a popular venue for meetings, concerts and boxing matches, and is also famous for hosting the **Last Night of the Proms**, an annual series of classical concerts. On the other side of the road is the **Albert Memorial**, another elaborate remembrance to **Prince Albert**, who organised the 1851 Great Exhibition.

Serpentine Gallery, Hyde Park

Exhibition Road is home to perhaps the greatest concentration of museums in any city. These museums were among the first to develop child-friendly, inter-active displays and millions of British children have received a major part of their education here. Their names are self-explanatory. The **Museum of Instruments** is part of the **Royal College of Music**. The **Science Museum** has an interesting display of vintage cars, not to mention **Alexander Bell**'s first telephone. The **Natural History Museum** is famous for its dinosaur exhibits and is linked to the **Geological Museum**. Opposite in **Cromwell Gardens** is the **Victoria and Albert Museum**, which specialises in the decorative arts. Its 11km of galleries has gold, silver, metal and woodwork, textiles, ceramics, glass and pottery from around the world and across the centuries. **The Dress Court** is a notable exhibition of European clothing from medieval times to the present. The **Photographic Gallery** has alternating exhibits from its archive of 300,000 British photographs dating back to 1856.

In the triangle between Kensington Road and Brompton Road is a well-preserved series of **Georgian squares** interspersed with lanes of quaint mews cottages. Hanging baskets, window boxes and pastel-coloured buildings in streets such as **Rutland Mews**, **Rutland Street** and **Fairholt Street**, create the impression of being in a peaceful rural Cornish fishing village rather than a bustling city centre.

If you don't fancy braving the tube and would rather sit back and be chauffeur driven between the sights, **OTR Minicoaches** operate a fleet a luxury, air-conditioned vehicles for corporate or private hire.

THE BRITISH LIBRARY
96 Euston Road, London NW1
Nearest Tube/Railway Stations:
King's Cross, St Pancras & Euston
Tel: 020 7412 7332
Email: visitor-services@bl.uk
Web: www.bl.uk

Britain today is a cultural "melting pot". Home to 3 exhibition Galleries, the British Library showcases documents and literature from a rich and diverse past. Find a wealth of cultures from all over the globe under one roof. Items range from original Beatles manuscripts to the Lindisfarne Gospels.

GLEN PORTCH
3 Bellring Close
Belvedere
Kent
DA17 6LP
Tel: (+44) 07949 185140
Email: glenp@tinyworld.co.uk
Web: www.walklondon.net

Gren Tours - Your Personal Bluebadge Guide to London. Museum and Gallery tours. Walking tours include Jack the Ripper, Royal London, Rock & Roll London and Pub Walks. Chauffeur guides available for tours of London, Oxford, Stratford, Bath, Stonehenge and more.

MUSEUM OF THE ORDER OF ST JOHN
St John's Gate, St John's Lane
Clerkenwell, London EC1M 4DA
Tel: 020 7324 4070
Fax: 020 7336 0587
Email: museum@nhq.sja.org.uk
Web: www.sja.org.uk/museum

Discover the History of the Knights Hospitaller at St John's Gate. Open: Mon-Fri 10am–5pm Sat 10am–4pm. Tours: Tues, Fri & Sat 11am & 2.30pm. Also, join us at the Living Museum in St James' Park from 4th–10th July.

THE NATURAL HISTORY MUSEUM
Cromwell Road
London
SW7 7BD
Tel: 020 7942 5000
Web: www.nhm.ac.uk

This world-class museum, holding over 70 million specimens from all over the globe, is dedicated to the fantastic story of our planet. Take an unforgettable journey into the Earth's past, present and future and discover its many natural wonders.

NATIONAL PORTRAIT GALLERY
St Martin's Place, London WC2H 0HE
Open daily 10am–6pm Thursday and Friday until 9pm
Admission Free
Nearest Public Transport: Leicester Square Tube
Tel: 020 7312 2463
Web: www.npg.org.uk

The National Portrait Gallery houses the finest collection of portraits in the world, offering a unique insight into the people who have shaped British culture. Featuring some of the most iconic and instantly recognisable faces in British history, from Elizabeth I to The Beatles and David Beckham, the National Portrait Gallery has something for everyone.

O.T.R. MINICOACHES
Waring House, Waring Street
London SE27 9LH
Tel: 0800 980 04 82 (FREEPHONE)
Fax: 0870 770 2474
Email: sales@otrtravel.com
Web: www.otrtravel.com

We operate a fleet of luxury air-conditioned chauffeur driven 7, 12, 16, 22 & 29 seater minibuses and mini-coaches for corporate/private/contract hire, as well as airport transfers, business trips, sightseeing tours in and around London. All vehicles are fitted with seatbelts and are less than 3 years old.

TOWER BRIDGE EXHIBITION
Tower Bridge
London
SE1 2UP
Tel: 020 7403 3761
Web: www.towerbridge.org.uk
Nearest tube - Tower Hill

Tower Bridge Exhibition allows visitors to witness stunning views of London from inside the high level walkways, read about the significance of the views and learn about the history and workings of this world-famous landmark. You are also able to see the original lifting machinery in the Victorian Engine Rooms.

WINSTON CHURCHILL'S BRITAIN AT WAR EXPERIENCE
Close to London Bridge Station
64/66 Tooley Street SE1 2TF
Tel: 0207 403 3171
Email: info@britainatwar.org.uk
Web: www.britainatwar.co.uk

An educational adventure to experience what life was like during the Second World War in war-torn Britain. This is a unique museum of interest to all ages, featuring evacuation, rationing, shelters, weddings, bomb disposal and gas masks. Walk through the London blitz. See it! Feel it! Breathe it! Open every day except 24–26 December.

Greater London is a massive metropolis and most of its attractions are found in the ancient cities of Westminster and London. But there are other places worth visiting and many of them are closely associated with the River Thames.

Greenwich

Royal connections with the river are strong. **Greenwich,** on the south-east bank of the Thames, was at the centre of British seafaring from the reign of King Henry VIII in the sixteenth century until the mid-nineteenth century, when the British Empire was at its height. The historic old town is a grand celebration of the nation's naval heritage where museums and royal homes compete with famous ships, book shops and markets for your attention. The town is dominated by the **Royal Naval College**, built by Sir Christopher Wren on the site of Henry's favourite palace, and has been the training school for generations of the Royal Navy's officers ever since. Beautifully landscaped gardens separate the college from the **Queen's House**, built by Inigo Jones in 1637 and once the home of **Henrietta Maria**, queen of the executed King Charles I. The main hall is a perfect cube, measuring 12m in each dimension.

The *Cutty Sark,* last of the Tea Clippers

Greenwich Meantime Clock

Nearby is the **National Maritime Museum,** where the numerous exhibits associated with the sea include the uniform worn by Admiral Lord Nelson when he died during the **Battle of Trafalgar** in 1805. Nearer the bank of the river are ***Gipsy Moth IV***, the tiny yacht sailed single-handedly round the world by **Sir Francis Chichester** in 1966-67, and the ***Cutty Sark***, the most famous of the nineteenth-century clippers which raced from the Far East to satisfy Britain's obsession with tea. **Greenwich Mean Time** (GMT) is the world basis for measuring time and the meridian 0º longitude, which divides the eastern and western hemispheres, passes through the **Old Royal Observatory** in Greenwich Park. The Astronomer Royal worked here from 1675 until 1948 and the Wren-designed building now houses a famous display of clocks and astronomical instruments.

Kew

Follow the river upstream to the west, perhaps using one of the many river launches which still ply their trade on the Thames, and you will reach **Kew Gardens,**

River Thames Barrier

officially called the **Royal Botanical Gardens**. The gardens, a World Heritage Site, are home to the world's leading botanical research centre, as well as being a popular attraction for visitors and Londoners alike. They were first laid out by **Capability Brown** in 1759 and more than 40,000 different kinds of plants are now on display in the manicured gardens and in the two huge Victorian glasshouses. The redbrick **Kew Palace** was where 'mad' **King George III** spent much of his time in the late-eighteenth century.

To the south of Kew Gardens is **Richmond Park**, a seventeenth-century royal hunting park in which the deer now graze untroubled apart from the thousands of Londoners who regularly enjoy the 660 hectares of heath and woodland. On the other side of Petersham Road is the stunning **Ham House**, one of the finest mansions in Britain which was once the home of the Duke of Lauderdale, confidant of King Charles II in the late-seventeenth century.

Hampton Court

Hampton Court, a former royal palace, is further upstream on the north bank, east of **Kingston upon Thames**. It was a favourite home for the Tudor and

Hampton Court garden entrance

Stuart kings and queens and has been open to the public since Victorian times. The magnificence of the palace is matched by its manicured gardens, created by Sir Christopher Wren, who included the famous **Maze**, in which many an unsuspecting visitor has since become lost. The building itself was twice rebuilt and extended and as a result is a pleasing mix of Tudor and English Baroque. **Anne Boleyn's Gateway** has an astronomical clock made for Henry VIII in 1540 above its entrance. Anne was one of the queens later executed by Henry.

Windsor

Still further upstream is the town of **Windsor**, dominated by the 900-year-old stone castle which has been fully restored following the fire of 1992. The castle is the Royal Family's summer residence; the royal standard flies from the **Round Tower** when the Queen is at home. On display in its many towers and

Windsor Castle

beautifully panelled halls are a golden shield presented to Henry VIII by **Francis I** of France and drawings and paintings from the important royal collection, including works by Holbein, da Vinci, Canaletto, Rubens and Rembrandt.

There are also exhibitions of antique furniture, tapestries, weapons, armour and military relics. The town of Windsor, a maze of half-timbered buildings, narrow lanes and cobbled streets, nestles in the shadows of the castle. At the north end of Windsor Bridge is the village of **Eton**, famous for its private school, **Eton College**, which has produced so many of Britain's military, political and business leaders. Windsor makes an enjoyable day-trip from London and can also be reached by train from Paddington Station. Alternatively, **Anderson Tours** provides a more luxurious way of travelling, with frequently scheduled bus tours to Windsor, Eton and beyond every week. All of its tours are guided, with packages to suit either the independent day-tripper or the longer-staying group.

The Crooked Tea Rooms and Carpenters Arms, Windsor

Hampstead

Rising high above north London is **Hampstead Heath**, a haven of woods, heathland, ponds and lakes offering spectacular views over the whole city. The heath has been a popular recreation area for Londoners for centuries and is a popular meeting place for courting couples. Music concerts are held at the Concert Pond, visitors can swim in the Ladies' Pond or Men's Pond and there are fairs several times a year. **Kenwood House**, on Hampstead Lane at the northern edge of the heath, has an art collection housing works by Vermeer, Rembrandt, Reynolds, Gainsborough and Van Dyck. A few hundred metres to the west at the top of Spaniards Road is the **Spaniards Inn**, where **Dick Turpin**, the infamous eighteenth-century highwayman, is said to have stayed.

Hampstead itself is one of the few old villages that has managed to keep its distinct historic identity intact within modern London. In recent times, Hampstead has been associated with the liberal left of politics and, particularly, Prime Minister Tony Blair's New Labour party. But the village has always been a centre for the famous; former residents include **Charles de Gaulle**, **Sigmund Freud**, writers **DH Lawrence** and **George Orwell**, poet **John Keats** and artist **John Constable**, who included the heath in some of his paintings.

Georgian and Regency architecture is everywhere. **Church Row**, near Hampstead railway station, is reckoned the finest Georgian Street in London. At the west end is **St John's Church**, where Constable's grave can be seen in the churchyard. **Fenton House**, on Hampstead Grove, dates from a slightly earlier period. The **Hampstead Museum** in Burgh House, on New End Square, has displays detailing the history of the village, as well as sections on Lawrence, Keats and Constable.

Oxford Street

London's West End is famed for the quality and variety of its shops and markets. If anything is made anywhere in the world, you can probably buy it in the department stores of Oxford Street, the designer shops of Regent Street, or on the stalls of Portobello Market or in any of the other retail areas in the city. National and international high street chains such as **Topshop, H&M, Monsoon, Zara, Next,** and **Oasis** are everywhere but even designer names such as **Armani, Louis Vuitton** or **Cartier** may have a shop in each of the main shopping streets, as well as concessions in larger department stores.

Leicester Square, Switzerland tourist shop

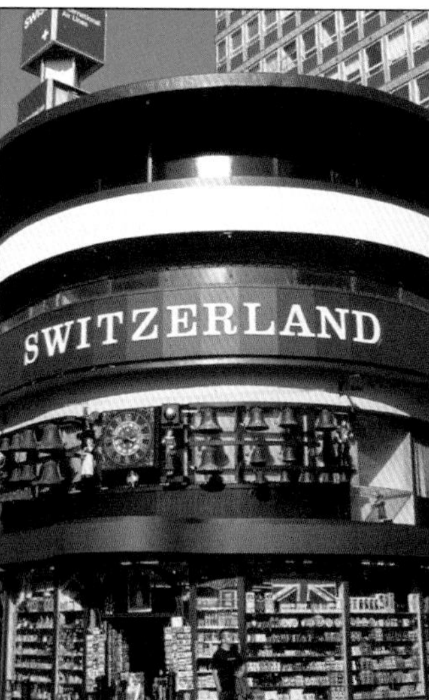

Oxford Street is dominated by large department stores, the best known being **Selfridge's,** which has top fashion ranges, and **John Lewis,** which sells fabrics, china, glass and household items. **Marks & Spencer,** the favourite department store of middle England, has two large shops on Oxford Street, one near Marble Arch and the other east of Oxford Circus.

No 1 Poultry is one of the leading postmodern buildings in London

Although M&S has diversified and now caters for home interiors, fashion for all the family remains its main business.

South of Oxford Street you will find the more expensive shopping areas of **Regent Street**, **Bond Street** and **Piccadilly**. Regent Street's sweeping terraced shops play host to top names in design for both men and women, from **Aquascutum**, **Austin Reed**, **Burberry**, and **Jaeger** to **Dickins & Jones** (housing top labels such as Donna **Karan**, **Paul Smith** and **Valentino**) and **Laura Ashley**. **Liberty**, with its Tudor-style exterior and wood-panelled interior, is famous for its signature floral printing on a range of furniture and fabrics. In the same precinct there is a large Next outlet, as well as **Hamley's**, still the greatest toy shop in Britain, from where generations of children have received teddy bears, train sets and every other kind of toy. **Tower Records**, near the Piccadilly Circus junction, has a huge selection of music across all genres, while **Lillywhite's** is the only sports department store in Britain.

Off Regent Street is **Savile Row,** a name synonymous with expert English tailoring. **Gieves & Hawkes** is the classic old-school gentleman's tailor. **Richard James** is more adventurous in terms of style and fabrics. The top of **Bond Street** (New Bond Street) is tag-hag heaven. **Versace, Bally, D&G, Pal Zileri, Nicole Farhi, Armani** and **Mulberry** all have stores selling the latest catwalk fashions, while **Fenwick** is a department store selling quality giftware and clothing for men and women at reasonable prices.

Further south on Bond Street is a cluster of expensive jewellery and watch shops, including **Gucci, Rolex, Patek Philippe** and **Watches of Switzerland**. **Cartier** and **Asprey & Garrard,** the Royal jewellers, are shops where

Harrod's façade, Knightsbridge

prices for designer jewellery go as high as you can afford. **De Beers**, the world's leading diamond merchant, is on the corner of Piccadilly. **Sotheby's**, the famous auction house, is also on Bond Street, with its biggest competitor, **Christie's**, on the other side of Piccadilly on King Street.

St James's Street, which runs between Piccadilly and Pall Mall, is a Mecca for cigar smokers. **Davidoff** is at No. 35; while at No. 19 is **Fox's**, supplier of Winston Churchill's famous Romeo Y Julietta cigars and the only cigar shop with a Royal Warrant from the Queen. **Claridge's Hotel**, just north on Brooke Street, has a smoking room ('fumoir') where twenty different types of Cuban cigars are on sale. On St James's Street you will also find **John Lobb**, the Royal Family's cobbler whose handmade shoes cost around £1,500 a pair and take six months to be made and delivered, while nearby you can find **James Lock,** a milliner which has been selling hats since the eighteenth century.

On Piccadilly is **Fortnum and Mason**, where food is more than just fuel, it's a religion. Knightsbridge is home to Britain's best-known shop, **Harrod's**, which once boasted to be able to supply anything asked of it, including, supposedly, an Indian elephant for one customer. The twice-yearly sales – New Year and summer – are occasions when you can find genuine bargains. Even if the giant department store is a bit more customary in what it sells these days, you can still buy everything from an AAA battery to Beluga caviar, from the latest CD to a grand piano, and ambling through its three hundred departments remains the greatest shopping or browsing experience in London.

The splendidly tiled **Food Hall** now caters more for the lunchtime takeaway trade (such as filled baguettes and bagels, Indian samosas and sushi) but still has seemingly endless traditional ranges of cheese, cooked meats, teas, coffees and other delicacies on display. You can also eat at a sushi bar or the cheese and wine bar, or try the small **Gentleman's Pub** in the basement. Also in Knightsbridge is **Harvey Nichols**, otherwise known as 'Harvey Nics', beloved of rock stars, high-earning footballers and Victoria Beckham. **Tiffany**, the jeweller, is on **Sloane Square,** while **Monolo Blahnik**'s stilettos can be found tottering away in nearby **Old Church Street**. Irish designer **Louise Kennedy** has a shop in West Halkin Street, near Belgrave Square.

King's Road is still fashionable, with a large number of small boutiques and chains to be found along it, one of which is **Habitat,** founded by lifestyle guru Sir Terence Conran. **Covent Garden** has numerous small specialist shops, such as **The Covent Garden Candle Company** and **Neal's Yard Dairy**, which sells farmhouse cheese supplied by Britain's growing number of small family-run manufacturers.

Other areas specialise in particular types of shops. **Charing Cross Road** is famous for its bookshops, where you'll be able to find old or new editions or specific titles. **Carnaby Street**, where the 'Swinging London' of the 1960s started, is now largely occupied by mid-range boutiques and chain stores. **Pimlico Road** is a centre for antique furnishings and prints and also houses **Linley**, the furniture shop owned and supplied by Viscount Linley, the Queen's nephew.

Markets

London markets are still thriving despite competition from the high street and American-style shopping malls in the suburbs. They're lively and fun, full of bargains and each with its own unique character.

Shepherd's Bush Market on Goldhawk Road has stall-holders whose humorous repartee is a free variety

Covent Garden, Apple Market

show in itself. On sale are household and electrical goods, fabric, West Indian foods and Asian spices, all reflecting the ethnic mix of the local community. **Portobello Road Market** is famous for its antiques and bric-a-brac, with more than 200 stalls selling objets d'art, jewellery, paintings, silverware and fruit and vegetables. The best stalls are at the Notting Hill end. **Camden Lock Market** gets crowded at the weekend, thronged by younger people looking to buy new and second-hand clothes, records, books and craftwork. **Camden Passage Market** is a quieter affair, where you can slowly sift through prints, silverware and jewellery. **Petticoat Lane Market** on Middlesex Street is probably the best known of London's markets, selling clothes, leather, jewellery and toys. **Old Spitalfields Market** specialises in street fashion and many of today's trendy young designers have started off selling their gear here. Best to go on Sundays. Other regular markets are held at **Brick Lane, Bermondsey** (Long Lane), **Berwick Street, Brixton, Southwark** (Borough Market), **Chapel Market, Church Street, Columbia Road** (Shoreditch), **East Street** (Elephant & Castle), **Greenwich, Leadenhall, Leather Lane, Ridley Road** and **St Martin-in-the-Fields**.

Savoy Hotel overlooking the Thames

Hotel rooms in London are expensive when compared with other European cities but, with a bit of research and planning, it is possible to get good accommodation near the centre at a reasonable price. Hotels are rated from one- to five-star in terms of luxury by the London Tourist Board. The luxury hotels are just that: opulent five-star wonders with liveried doormen and every kind of electronic gadget and variety of soft towels in your room. But, if you are spending your days sight-seeing and only returning to sleep, something lower down the price scale may be more appropriate.

For those travelling to or from **Stansted Airport**, the **Radisson SAS** is in a great location, offering value for money with various amenities that include gym,

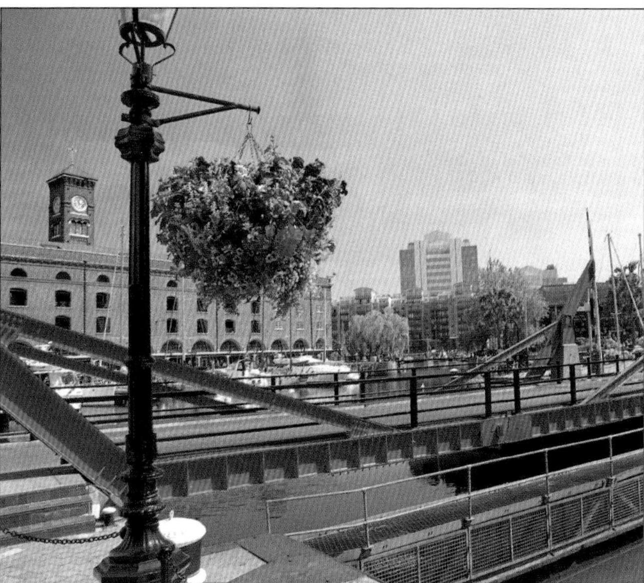

Tower Hotel, St Catherine's docks

swimming pool and aerobic studios. Also offering a base for the traveller, the **Harlow/Stansted Moat House** is ideal for business or leisure activities, with all the desired facilities and with shopping and direct access routes to the city centre in close proximity. Alternatively, check out the **Stansted Manor Hotel**, which offers ease of travel coupled with a peaceful night's sleep in the hotel's secluded country setting.

If all you want during your stay is a room and a shower, chains such as **Novotel**, **Ibis** and **Holiday Inn** have generic branches all around the city. Look up their websites for locations. Remember, there can be wide variations in prices between hotels and often something less expensive might provide you with all the comfort you need.

Check if you are being charged per room or per person. Also, most hotels charge for rooms only, so ask whether breakfast is included. This may be anything from a calorie-laden fry-up or a full buffet to simple cereal and toast, depending on the hotel. Make sure your quoted price includes VAT and other charges. All hotels accept major credit cards. Prices are very much governed by supply and demand, so it makes sense to shop around, particularly on the Internet, and to ask for a discount. Prices range from £100-£150 per night for a mid-range hotel room to more than £250 at the five-star end. Cheaper hotels should cost £80 or less. You do not need to tip, except perhaps for porters in the more up-market hotels, but, of course, you can always be nice and tip where deserved.

Ritz Hotel in Piccadilly

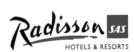

The cheapest rooms are usually in **B&Bs** (bed and breakfasts) which are a British holiday institution. Some are like small hotels and many are actually family homes where some rooms have been converted for guests. The breakfasts are usually wholesome and substantial. Some rooms in older hotels and B&Bs may not have en-suite bathrooms.

There are a number of hostels in the centre. The **Oxford Street Hostel** is in Noel Street, in the heart of the city in Soho, while **Holland House** is a seventeenth-century Jacobean mansion in Holland Park in West London. Three agencies handle hostel bookings: **International Booking Network, London Hostel Association** and **Youth Hostels Association.** You can also rent rooms in student halls of residence during university vacations; three that provide this service are **City University, Imperial College** and **King's College**.

Accommodation is also generally cheaper the further you go from the city centre. Most suburban centres, such as Ealing, Wembley, Edgware, or Finchley, have a ready supply of hotels and B&Bs, as well as good transport links. But if you're looking for something right in the heart of the city **Europa House Hotel** is a comfortable, family-run B&B which has been in business since 1974 and is a great base for exploring the surrounding attractions.

Down towards Vauxhall on Ebury Street is **Morgan House**, a bright, eleven-room budget B&B located in a typical Georgian terrace and a stone's throw from the art and antique shops of Pimlico Road. Also in the same district in Victoria is **The Windermere Hotel**, a family-run business and recipient of various accolades where the staff treats its guests with intimate consideration and the professionalism of a large hotel. **Parkwood** is a pleasant, family-run B&B in Stanhope Place, just by Marble Arch. Around the corner in

Marble Arch

Seymour Street is the **Edward Lear**, a B&B in the former restored Georgian home of Edward Lear, the famous Victorian humorist and inventor of limerick poems. Nearer to Paddington Station (the mainline railway station serving Wales and the west of England) is Sussex Gardens, which has many budget guest houses and small hotels. The owners of the **Pavilion** clearly have fun in the hotel business if their eccentrically-themed bedrooms are anything to go by, while the **Delmere** is an outstanding hotel with Internet access in each of its thirty-six rooms.

In Gloucester Place you'll find the **Lincoln House Hotel**, an elegantly converted Georgian townhouse that has won awards for its superb floral displays. It also includes breakfast and service in its price. For similar luxury and value, **The Jenkins Hotel**, situated in the

famed Bloomsbury area of London, is another refurbished Georgian house that promises a personable and charming stay in historic surroundings.

La Gaffe, on Heath Street in the heart of Hampstead village in north London, is an Italian restaurant with rooms upstairs. The bedrooms are small but pretty and all are non-smoking – B&B prices in a fully-licensed hotel with Italian cuisine to boot! Nearby is the **Langdorf**, a 36-bedroom hotel made up of three converted townhouses. The hotel also has three self-catering apartments.

The Knightsbridge area to the south of Hyde Park is usually expensive but the **Claverley**, just a two-minute walk from Harrod's in Beaufort Gardens, is regularly rated one of the best value B&Bs in London. Try to get one of the first floor rooms, with their floor-to-ceiling windows and four-poster beds. **The Basil Street Hotel**, long-established and popular with the ladies, is also near Knightsbridge tube station. **The Willett** is an elegant red-brick B&B whose room rates are surprisingly low for the location in Sloane Gardens near Sloane Square (spiritual home of the 'Sloane Rangers', the young upper-class who typified the pleasure-seeking London of the 1980s). Nearby is the chic Duke of York Square shopping area with boutiques selling high-fashion clothing, shoes, jewellery and trendy furniture.

If money is no object, the **Mayfair** and **St. James's** areas probably have more luxury hotels per square kilometre than any other part of London. The best known is **Claridge's** on Brook Street, an art deco palace frequented by A-list celebrities; former professional footballer-turned-superstar chef Gordon Ramsay has a highly rated restaurant here. **Brown's** is a traditional hotel which occupies eleven former townhouses on Albermarle Street and has a gym and swimming pool.

On into Piccadilly is **22 Jermyn Street**, which has use of one of the best health clubs in London and provides fresh flowers for every room. Jermyn Street is famous for its gentleman's tailors and made-to-measure shirts and shoes. And there is always the **Ritz** on Piccadilly, the swankiest of the swanky London hotels, complete with Louis XIV furnishings and other extravagant fixtures that have decorated the classy hotel since its opening 100 years ago. **Hazlitt's**, further north on Frith Street in the heart of Soho, occupies three eighteenth-century houses. Its panelled walls, paintings and antique Victorian furnishings make it a favourite with the artistic community. Scarcely less expensive in the area north of Oxford Street is the Marylebone railway station hotel, **The Landmark**. This hotel has a spectacular eight-storey-high atrium full of palm trees and was once the headquarters of the British Railways Board. Facilities include a pool, sauna, gym and Turkish bath.

If you plan on spending time visiting the museums around Kensington, which include the Victoria and Albert Museum, the Science Museum and the Natural History Museum, the **Bayswater Inn** is ideally located on Princes Square, and offers its guests a cosy coffee shop and restaurant in which to refuel and, if that doesn't do it, the late-serving bar might! **The Residence**, on Old Brompton Road, has modern self-catering mini-apartments for rent not far from Gloucester Road tube station. Nearby, **Five Sumner Place**, just off the Fulham Road in South Kensington, has won a number of tourism awards for accommodation and is a great base from which to check out the surrounding area and beyond. Prices for this comfortable Victorian house are very reasonable. If you fancy a late-night pint, the

Waterloo Station

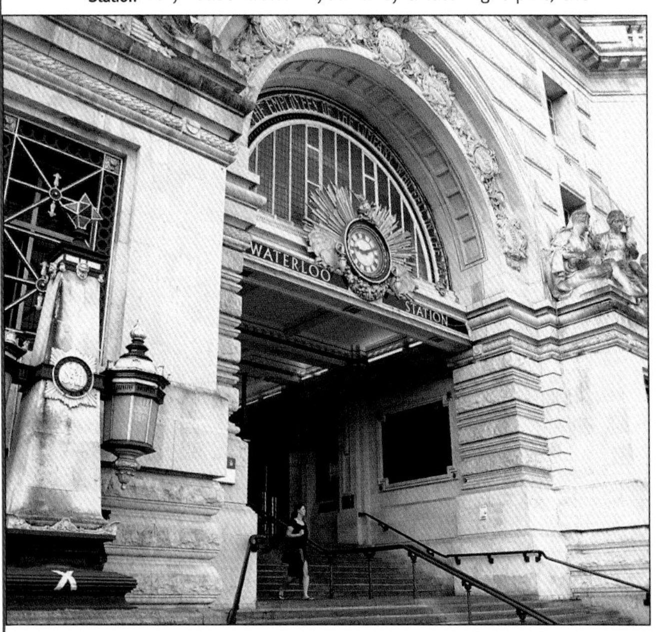

atmospheric **Anglesea Arms** pub is 400 metres away on Selwood Terrace. Also providing you with the opportunity to check out the restaurants and pubs nearby is **Hotel 65**, a delightful enterprise offering comfort and value for money.

There are fewer budget hotels to the east and southeast of the city centre, although **The Fielding** in Bow Street, near The Strand, is recommended. Further out at Greenwich, the **Ibis Greenwich** is cheap and cheerful and easily accessible to the city on the Docklands Light Railway. **The Mitre** on Greenwich High Road is an old eighteenth-century coffee house turned into a busy, good-value inn with sixteen rooms. The classiest and most expensive of the hotels in the east is the exclusive 142-room **Four Seasons Canary Wharf**, set right in the heart of the Canary Wharf docklands development. It has superb waterfront views of the Thames and mainly serves business people, although it also caters for families.

South of the river, near the London Eye, the **Travel Inn** on Belvedere Road proves there's always a use for redundant buildings in London, occupying as it does the converted headquarters of the Greater London Council, which was abolished by Margaret Thatcher in 1986.

The Novotel Waterloo is a large mid-price chain hotel not far from Waterloo Station. **Aconflag** is a well-established small hotel on Clapham Common South Side in south London whose owners recently bought the **Quality Hotel Crystal Palace**.

Finally, **Euro Hotels** has accommodation in all corners of London. Hotels to the southwest of the city include: **Euro Hotels Clapham**, which is located on Clapham Common Southside and has on-site parking; the thirty-nine room **Cavendish Lodge** on Cavendish Road, just around the corner, has a TV and a direct-dial telephone in every room; and, on the northside of the common, **Gilmore House** contains serviced apartments which are available for long- or short-term lets. In the southeast of the city, the **Peckham Lodge** is only ten minutes walk from access to the East London Underground Line, and **Queens Hotel**, south of here in Crystal Palace, is in a refurbished Victorian building, only five minutes walk from the Crystal Palace Sports Centre. Further south again, in Croydon, the **Norfolk House Hotel** and the **Dunheved Hotel** can be found on London Road. Both hotels have en-suite facilities, TVs and direct-dial telephones, while the Norfolk House Hotel has a bar and restaurant open seven days a week. In Wembley, in the northwest corner of the city, you'll find the **Elm Hotel**. Built in 1898, the Elm is the oldest hotel in Wembley and has a family room which can sleep up to six people. The **Kenton House Hotel**, also near Wembley, is conveniently located for visitors requiring easy access to central London; the hotel is just ten minutes walk from Hanger Lane tube station on the Central Line. Also on the Central Line in Leytonstone in Northeast London is the **Sleeping Beauty Motel** on Lea Bridge Road. If you're on your way in or out of London by air, Euro Hotels also have the **Channins Hounslow Hotel** near Heathrow Airport and the **Hunters Lodge Hotel** close to Gatwick.

BAYSWATER INN 8-16 Princes Square London W2 4NT Tel: 0207 792 3536 Fax: 0207 727 3346 Email: reservations@bayswaterinn.co.uk Web: www.bayswaterinn.co.uk	The refurbished London 3-star standard Bayswater Inn has 139 bedrooms en-suite with tea and coffee making facilities, telephone, television and hairdryer. Two lifts, Bar and Coffee Shop. Located in residential square close to Queensway, with its variety of restaurants and Whiteley's Shopping Centre, Portobello Market, Hyde Park, Oxford Street and the West End.
CAVENDISH LODGE 41/43/45 Cavendish Road London SW12 0BH Tel: 020 8772 1222 Fax: 020 8772 1333 Email: office@europroperties.co.uk	Located just off Clapham Common 10 minutes walk to Clapham south tube station which is fifteen minutes to central London. Some rooms with en-suite facilities, featuring TV, direct-dial telephone.
CHANNINS HOUNSLOW HOTEL 41 Hounslow Road Feltham Middlesex TW14 0AU Tel: 020 8890 2358/020 8831 0688 Fax: 020 8751 6103	Located ten minutes from Heathrow Airport (Bus 285 from Feltham Park to Central Bus Terminal at Heathrow) and thirty minutes to Waterloo with a direct train from Feltham Station. Rooms are all en-suite and feature colour TV, direct-dial telephone and tea and coffee facilities.
DUNHEVED HOTEL 639-641 London Road Thornton Heath CR7 6AZ Tel: 020 8684 2009 Fax: 020 8240 1133 Email: office@europroperties.co.uk	Located in Croydon. Situated just 10 minutes walk from Crystal Palace sports centre. All rooms with en-suite facilities, featuring TV, direct-dial telephone.
ELM HOTEL 1-11 Elm Road Wembley Middlesex HA9 7JA Tel: 020 8902 1764 Fax: 020 8903 8365	Located 7 minute walk from Wembley Central. 20 minutes travel to central London. Close to Wembley stadium. All rooms have en-suite facilities, featuring TV, direct-dial telephone.
EURO HOTELS CLAPHAM 80-81 Clapham Common South Side London SW4 9DL Tel: 020 8673 3534/0208772 1234 Fax: 020 8675 1100 Email: office@europroperties.co.uk	Located in the open space of Clapham Common, 5 minutes walk to Clapham south tube station which is fifteen minutes to central London. All rooms have en-suite facilities, featuring TV, direct-dial telephone and some are equipped with a mini fridge.

EUROPA HOUSE HOTEL
151 Sussex Gardens
Hyde Park
London W2 2RY
Tel: 020 7723 7343
Fax: 020 7224 9331
Email: europahouse@enterprise.net
Web: www.europahousehotel.com

The Europa House is a family-run Bed & Breakfast since 1974. Situated in the heart of London, all rooms are en-suite with telephone, TV, and tea/coffee making facilities. The surrounding area offers a large selection of restaurants and pubs, London Theatreland and Madame Tussauds. Easy access to Gatwick, Heathrow Express and Stansted Express.

FIVE SUMNER PLACE HOTEL
5 Sumner Place
South Kensington
London SW7 3EE
Tel: 020 7584 7586
Fax: 020 7823 9962
Email: reservations@sumnerplace.com
Web: www.sumnerplace.com

Awarded "Best Small Hotel". This family owned and run hotel offers excellent service and personal attention. All rooms are with private facilities, voicemail and Free Fast Internet Access WiFi. The hotel is ideally located for sightseeing or business.

GILMORE HOUSE
113 Clapham Common North Side
London SW4 9SN
Tel: 020 7228 1415
Fax: 020 7228 1416
Email: office@europroperties.co.uk

Serviced apartments available for short or long term lets. Located in Clapham Common Northside.
Prices from £125 per week.

HARLOW/STANSTED MOAT HOUSE HOTEL
Southern Way
Harlow, Essex
CM 18 7BA
Tel: 01279 829988
Fax: 01279 829906

The Harlow/Stansted Moat House Hotel, with its 119 en-suite bedrooms and great location, is the ideal venue for all your requirements. With fantastic conference and exhibition space; stay before you fly packages and great leisure club facilities.
For a virtual tour of the hotel please visit www.moathousehotels.com.

HUNTERS LODGE HOTEL
Nutfield Road
Redhill
Surrey RH1 4EB
Tel: 01737 778 190
Fax: 01737 789 082
Email: office@europroperties.co.uk

Located in Redhill. 10 minutes by car to Gatwick airport. All rooms have en-suite facilities, featuring TV, and direct-dial telephone. Close to all local amenities and transport links.

HOTEL 65
65 Shepherds Bush Road
Hammersmith
London W6 7LS
Tel: +44 (0) 207 603 5634
Fax: +44(0) 207 603 4933
Email: bookings@hotel65.com
Website: www.hotel65.com

Hotel 65 is a clean, friendly and comfortable family-run hotel. 5 minutes from underground, close to Hammersmith Apollo, Shepherds Bush Empire and within walking distance of good restaurants, pubs and the River Thames. Rooms are en-suite with TV and tea/coffee making facilities. 24-hour reception. Tariffs include full English breakfast and taxes.

THE JENKINS HOTEL 45 Cartwright Gardens Bloomsbury London WC1H 9EH Tel: 020 7387 2067 Fax: 020 7383 3139 Email: reservations@jenkinshotel.demon.co.uk Web: www.jenkinshotel.demon.co.uk	A small traditional family-run 18th-century Bed and Breakfast Hotel located in the city centre in a quiet crescent. All rooms have en-suite shower/WC, tea/coffee making facilities, TV, telephone, fridge, hairdryers and safes. All rooms are non-smoking. Tennis courts in the Gardens are available for guest's use.
KENTON HOUSE HOTEL 1-7 Hillcrest Road Ealing W5 2JL Tel: 020 8997 8436 Fax: 020 8998 0037 Email: office@europroperties.co.uk	Located 10 minutes walking to the tube station (Hanger Lane). Central London 15 minutes from the Central Line. All rooms have en-suite facilities, featuring TV, direct-dial telephone.
LINCOLN HOUSE HOTEL-Central London 33 Gloucester Place, Marble Arch London W1U 8HY Tel: + 44(0)20 74867630 Fax: +44(0)20 7486 0166 E: reservations@lincoln-house-hotel.co.uk Special Offers: www.lincoln-house-hotel.co.uk	A delightfully hospitable Georgian hotel, with modern comforts & en-suite rooms from £48 in the heart of London's West End. Close to most theatres, tourist attractions & designer shops of Oxford and Bond Streets. Free internet access. Commended by many travel guidebooks.
NORFOLK HOUSE HOTEL 587 London Road Thornton Heath CR7 6AY Tel: 020 8689 8989 Fax: 020 8689 0335 Email: office@europroperties.co.uk	Located in Croydon. 10 minutes walk from Crystal Palace sports centre. All rooms have en-suite facilities, featuring TV, direct-dial telephone. Bar and restaurant available 7 days a week
PECKHAM LODGE 110 Peckham Road London SE15 5AD Tel: 020 7701 4222 Fax: 020 7701 4555 Email: office@europroperties.co.uk	Located in Peckham. 10 minutes walk to tube station which is 20 minutes to central London. Some rooms with en-suite facilities, featuring TV, direct-dial telephone.
QUEENS HOTEL 122 Church Road Crystal Palace SE19 2UG Tel: 020 8653 6622 Fax: 020 8653 0404	Located in Crystal Palace, set in a Victorian building. The hotel is 5 minutes from Crystal Palace sports centre. All bedrooms are en-suite. Conference and Banqueting facilities from 2 to 550 guests.

RADISSON SAS HOTEL
LONDON STANSTED AIRPORT
Waltham Close, Essex, CM24 1PP
Tel: +44 (0) 1279 661012
Fax: +44 (0) 1279 661013
Email: info.stansted@radissonsas.com
Website: www.stansted.radissonsas.com

The Radisson SAS Hotel London Stansted Airport is an ultra modern contemporary styled hotel designed for both the business & leisure guest. With the diversity on offer and the unique Wine Tower as a focus, it is not only known as a place to sleep, it is the place to meet, eat and be entertained!

SLEEPING BEAUTY MOTEL
543 & 586 Lea Bridge Road
Leyton E10 7DN
Tel/Fax: 020 8556 8080
Email: office@europroperties.co.uk

Located in Leytonstone. Central London 25 minutes by Central Line. Fifteen minutes from central London. All rooms have en-suite facilities, featuring satellite TV, direct-dial telephone.

STANSTED MANOR HOTEL
Birchanger Lane
Birchanger
Essex
CM23 5ST
Tel: 01279 859 800
Email: info@stanstedmanor-hotel.co.uk

Stansted Manor Hotel is only 3 miles from the terminal building of Stansted Airport and within 1/2 mile of Junction 8 of the M11. With 70 large en-suite bedrooms, all of which are comfortably furnished and have high-speed Internet access. Wyndhams restaurant provides a comprehensive range of food throughout the day.

WINDERMERE HOTEL
142/144 Warwick Way
Victoria
London
SW1V 4JE
Tel: 020 7834 5163
Fax: 020 7630 8831
Email: reservations@windermere-hotel.co.uk
Web: www.windermere-hotel.co.uk

Winner of the "Best B&B, Visit London Tourism Awards 2003". Ideally located close to Victoria Station, with easy access to all London Airports. Close to Buckingham Palace, Westminster Abbey, Houses of Parliament, Tate Britain, the shops of Chelsea and Knightsbridge. Moderately priced, individually designed rooms, inclusive of our "famous" English breakfast.

For those looking for entertainment and excitement, London is one of the best places to be. Whether it's a bar or a band you're looking for, this city will undoubtedly offer up something to keep you amused. Extended pub opening hours has meant that the fun continues long into the night. Although many pubs still close at 11pm (they open at 11am), some have late licences and of course there's a booming club scene designed to keep you partying until dawn.

Pubs and bars

Some find that British beer (usually called 'bitter') is an acquired taste, but it's one worth acquiring. The best beer is cask-conditioned 'real' ale which is sold in most central pubs, a far-cry from twenty years ago when it was a rarity in many. Look for beer being served using a hand pump rather than a small keg tap – the first is real beer, the other is a tasteless, chemically-treated imitation. Beers brewed by London-based **Young's and Fuller's** are most common and among the best. Every pub, and many bars, will also sell Guinness, the dark

Royal Albert Hall

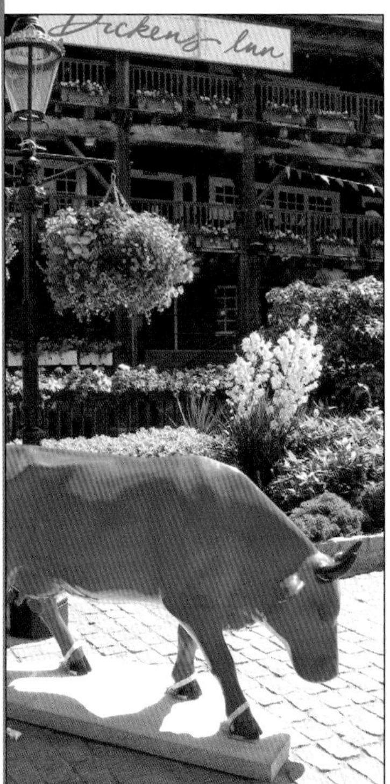

Dickens Inn

Irish stout which has been brewed in London for decades, and there's a wide range of British and European lagers, draught and bottled, also available.

Old riverside pubs are popular, particularly on sunny summer weekends. There are a number dotted along the winding curves of the Thames. **The Dove** near Hammersmith Bridge is a seventeenth-century maze of rooms, and it claims to include the smallest bar in the country. **The Anchor**, near Tate Modern, has three cosy bars. The 500-year-old **Prospect of Whitby** has stunning views of the north bank at Wapping, which belies its grim past as the setting for public executions, one victim of which was the notorious pirate Captain Kidd in 1701. **The Trafalgar Tavern** in Greenwich is a relative newcomer, built in 1837, but it boasts a rich literary history with authors Thackeray, Dickens and Wilkie Collins being regulars in the past. Another popular pub boasting a long history is the **Churchill Arms**, located across the river in Kensington, which serves both traditional and Thai food and has a pleasant beer garden for lazy, warm summer evenings.

The Sherlock Holmes in Charing Cross is a favourite with tourists, largely because of its association with Sir Arthur Conan Doyle, a former regular. There is a

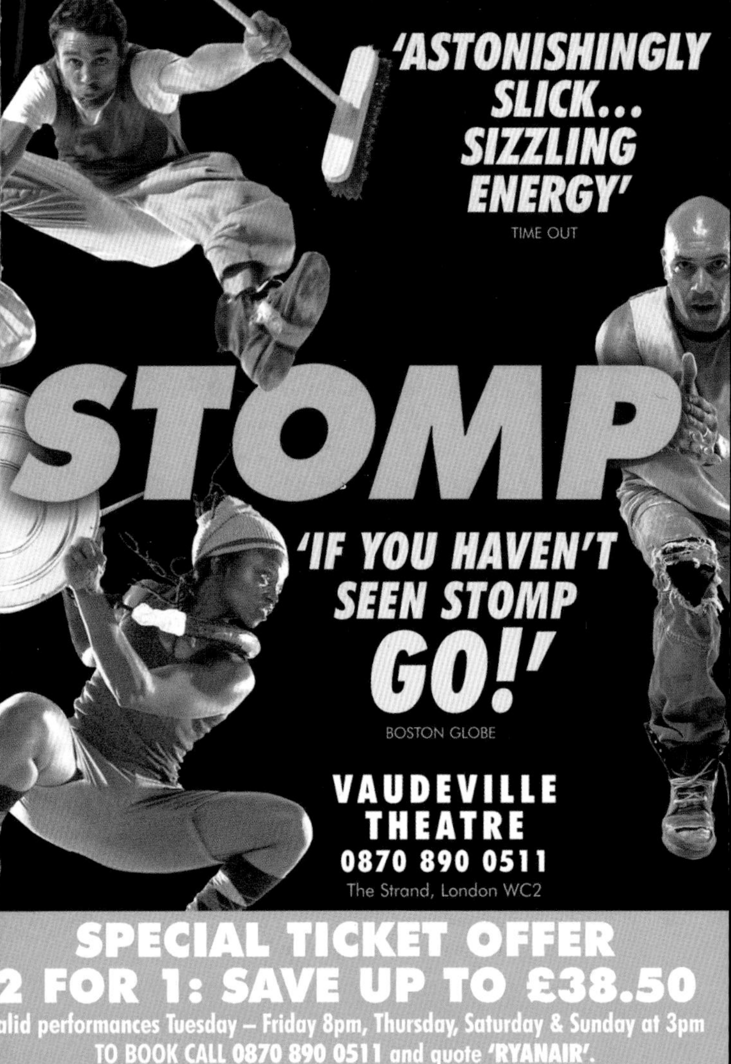

SPECIAL TICKET OFFER

2 FOR 1: SAVE UP TO £38.50

Valid performances Tuesday – Friday 8pm, Thursday, Saturday & Sunday at 3pm

TO BOOK CALL 0870 890 0511 and quote 'RYANAIR'.

Offer subject to availability, some exclusions may apply call box office for details.

Traditional pub in the city

collection of Holmes memorabilia and a reconstruction of Doyle's study. Also situated in Charing Cross is **The Harp Pub**, which offers tourist and regular alike a friendly, personable atmosphere, great beers, and wonderfully large windows that can be opened up on a warm summer's day. North of here, near Finsbury Park, **The Blarney Stone** has an equally warm ambience and two big-screen televisions.

For live acts in central London – be they rock 'n' roll or poetry recitals – **Filthy McNasty's Whiskey Café** on Amwell Street in Islington comes highly recommended. Parties of up to 120 people can be catered for. Another party venue catering for all kinds of occasions is the **London Irish Centre** in Camden Square. Even though it's right in the heart of London, the London Irish Centre has a peaceful garden and is ideal for conference, banqueting and cultural events.

QUOTE 'RYAN AIR' TO RECEIVE THESE SPECIAL OFFERS!

FAME
THE MUSICAL

TOP SEATS JUST £19.75
(normally £39.50)

CALL ALDWYCH THEATRE 0870 400 0805 NOW!

Not valid Fri 5.30pm + Sat 7.30pm performances. Subject to availability + bkg fee.
Cannot be used in conjunction with any other offers.

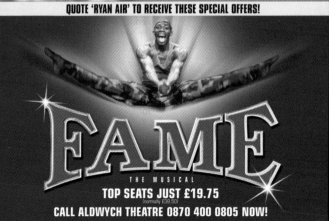

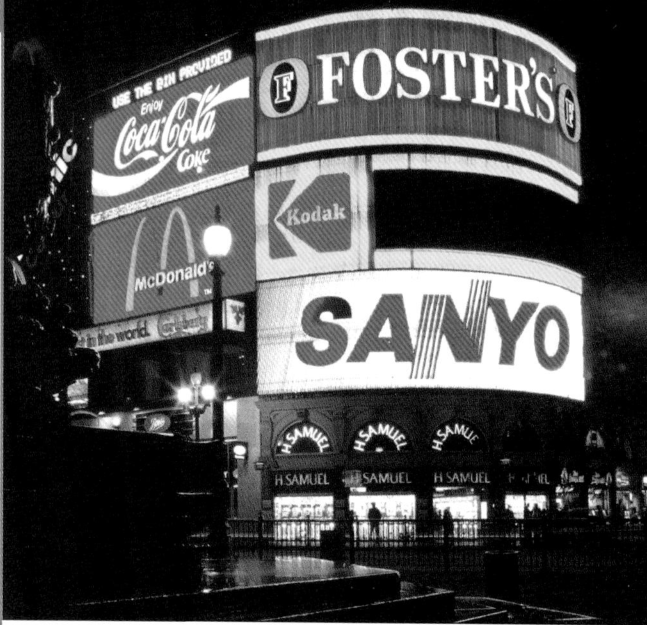

Piccadilly Circus, a hub of activity, particularly spectacular at night

If you're thinking of venturing out to the northwest of London and are looking for more Irish-themed entertainment, **The James Joyce** pub, located in Harrow, offers live entertainment and quiz nights in a fun-filled environment throughout the week. **The Welcome Inn** in Cricklewood is a more traditional Irish venue that's open late every evening. For really late opening hours, check out **Finbar's**, in Neasden, near Cricklewood, where the drink stays flowing till 5am. The pub also serves up fresh home-cooked food and has function rooms available. Two more venues sharing the same name are located in **Willesden** and on Edgware Road in **Colindale**, also in the northwest of the city. Both provide good food, great entertainment, and friendly staff, making your pub and dining experience a pleasant one.

National Theatre

'The National Theatre has become the place to be; seats for serious shows at low prices - half the price of a football match.'

Guardian

Tickets from £10

www.nationaltheatre.org.uk

020 7452 3000 The National Theatre is a registered charity

South Molton Street at night

There is no shortage of pubs in East London. The **Hammers Public House** is a traditional East End pub where **West Ham** fans congregate on match days. **Chevy Chase** and **Antelope Public House** can be found near Stratford; both serve up traditional Irish entertainment in the form of live music sessions and televised GAA matches respectively, while the **Earl of Essex** between Stratford and Ilford offers live music as well and is open until 2am at weekends. Also in the area, the family-run **Princess of Wales** on West Ham Lane serves food daily.

Gay & Lesbian Venues

There is a thriving gay and lesbian scene in and around Old Compton Street in Soho. **Compton's** is a lively pub, as is the better-known **The Admiral Duncan**. **Balans** does food and drinks. **The Edge** in Soho Square was originally 'men only' but has grown to attract both men and women, be they straight or gay. **The Candy Bar**

attracts a more lesbian crowd, while **The Fridge Bar** in Brixton Hill caters for women-only nights.

Clubs

The best known of the mainstream club/discos is **Stringfellows**. Owner Peter Stringfellow may conform to the ageing-trendy stereotype that does everything to excess but at least he doesn't take himself too seriously. He does, however, take his business seriously – it's still there in Charing Cross after all these years, still popular with locals and tourists alike, despite the prices. **The Hippodrome** on nearby Cranbourne Street is a fairly typical disco with a famous light show and a staggeringly loud sound system. **Trader Vic's** in the basement of the Hilton Hotel in Park Lane is Britain's only tiki bar: a cocktail bar with a Polynesian theme. Here you get the most extensive list of the most exotic cocktails at the most expensive of prices in the most kitsch of venues. It's well worth a visit.

Heaven is still the premier venue for house music, thanks to its easy-going style, large dance floor and pumping sound system. It attracts a mainly, but not exclusively, gay clientele to its location on Villiers Street. **Ministry of Sound** is probably more famous these days, thanks to the extensive marketing of its brand name. Famous DJs play house and garage sounds at the **Gaunt Street Club** at Elephant and Castle. **Fabric** in Smithfield is famous for playing alternative music which booms out through the floor of the 'Bodysonic' room. **Freedom Café** on Wardour Street in Soho is a coffee bar during the day and a trendy club at night. The patrons are a happy mix of straight and gay. The cutting-edge music crews may have moved on from the **Fridge Bar** on Brixton Hill but the venue is still hugely popular. There are several bars and a balcony which overlooks the dance floor, complete with cold air vents blast out cooling air – hence the club's name.

Jazz in London means **Ronnie Scott's** on Frith Street, Soho. The charismatic Mr Scott died some years ago having blown his last improvised saxophone solo but his club lives on, still attracting the top names in the jazz world after forty years. **The Pizza Express Jazz Club** nearby on Dean Street is exactly what its name says: a Pizza Express restaurant with added live jazz seven days a week in the basement. The pizza is what you would expect from the nationwide restaurant chain and the jazz is as excellent as you would expect from stars such as Mose Allison and Diana Krall. **The 100 Club** in Oxford was where the Sex Pistols played their first gig but the club is nowadays better known for its traditional jazz, particularly on Friday nights. **Bar Rumba** in Shaftesbury Avenue mixes acid jazz, salsa and house, depending on which night of the week it is, and has an early start (10 pm) by clubbing standards.

Theatres

The theatre has a long tradition in London, from Shakespeare's first nights at the **Globe** in the late sixteenth century to the modern musicals of **Andrew Lloyd-Webber** and **Cameron Mackintosh**. If you love plays or musicals then there's no chance of being bored in London, with more than thirty large commercial shows running at any one time in the West End alone. At the time of publication, three of the most popular **West End shows** are: **Fame**, full of unforgettable songs, dynamic dance routines and explosive vitality; the huge international hit **Stomp**, with its inventive use of everyday objects in a unique combination of

Apollo Theatre facade on Shaftesbury Avenue

irishbars.co.uk

Irishbars is a thriving Group of 14 London Irish Pubs. Offering a bright, friendly environment and centrally located they offer an enjoyable experience for all.
Big screens for sports coverage, traditional Irish music, live rock bands and no cover charge. Enjoy a night out in true Irish style! Recommended are The Welcome Inn, The James Joyce and Finabr's.

Irishbars.co.uk
225/227 Edgware Road
Colindale
London, NW9 6LU
Tel: 020 8200 5256
Fax: 020 8205 3088
Email:
johnmcgowan@irishbars.demon.co.uk
Web: www.irishbars.co.uk

Criterion Theatre

percussion, movement and visual comedy; and the legendary disco extravaganza **Saturday Night Fever**.

Modern theatre is divided between the state-subsidised national companies and the commercial sector. **The Royal National Theatre** is based in the **South Bank Centre**, where there are three theatres of different sizes presenting classic and modern plays, while the **Royal Shakespeare Company** regularly travels up from its base in Stratford-upon-Avon to play in the West End. There are also two theatres in the **Barbican Centre**.

Shaftesbury Avenue is at the heart of the commercial theatre district with five theatres and two cinemas. There are other clusters of theatres around Haymarket, Charing Cross Road and Aldwych. Many of the theatres have long histories – the **Theatre Royal Drury Lane** is the fourth on the site since 1663, when Nell Gwynne, the mistress of Charles II, acted there, while the **Savoy** is now where the D'Oyley Carte Company premiered Gilbert and Sullivan's light operas. The open-air Globe shows plays by Shakespeare and his contemporaries.

Fringe productions are staged upstairs in small theatres and pubs such as the **King's Head** in Islington, the **Latchmere** in Battersea and the **Prince Albert** in Notting Hill. The prestigious **Donmar Warehouse** off Shaftesbury Avenue is technically fringe but the number of stage and screen stars prepared to work there for basic union rates make it West End in practice (well, almost). **The Comedy Store** near Piccadilly Circus heralded the start of the comedy boom in the 1980s and remains a leading player. Musical concerts and opera are put on at a number of concert halls, large and small, across London. The main venues are the **Royal Albert Hall**, famous for hosting the **Proms** each summer, **Barbican Hall**, the **Royal Festival Hall**, **Wigmore Hall**, the **Royal Opera House** in Covent Garden, and the **London Coliseum**, home of the English National Opera. Ballet and modern dance venues include **Sadler's Wells** in Finsbury, the London Coliseum and the **Queen Elizabeth Hall** in the South Bank.

Tickets can be bought at the theatre box office in person or by telephone. Shows are often sold out months in advance but it is worth queuing on the night at the ticket office because there are usually returned

Theme boats on the Thames

FILTHY
MacNASTY'S

tickets available. In Leicester Square there's the **Half Price Theatre Ticket Booth** (TKTS), the only official outlet in the vicinity, where you can pick up tickets for a selection of West End shows at half the price.

Casinos

If you really want to experience some of the thrills of London nightlife you should check out one of the city's casinos. Two very popular ones are the **Palm Beach Casino** located on Berkeley Street and the **Mint Casino** on Cromwell Road, and both are entirely more sophisticated than any Las Vegas venture.

Cinemas

There is a healthy mix of commercial chains and independent ventures in London, with around fifty cinemas situated in central London and more than 200 in the surrounding area. This means that Londoners can catch the latest art-house flick, or any number of Hollywood's newest offerings. Well-known cinemas like the **Odeon** cater for such tastes, but to catch a less commercially-viable picture go to **Renoir** on Brunswick Square, the **Prince Charles** in Leicester Place or the **Curzon Soho** on Shaftesbury Avenue. The **London Film Festival**, held every October in many of the city's cinemas, is movie-buff heaven.

Live Music

London has always been a great base for the rise of music genres and the city homes a wide variety of bands – whether they be jazz and rock superstars or garage bands just starting out. Shows at big venues such as **Hammersmith Apollo**, the **London Arena** on the Isle of Dogs (12,500 capacity), or **Brixton Academy** book out well in advance but there are plenty of live bands playing everywhere from the back rooms of pubs to mid-size venues such as the **Mean Fiddler** on Charing Cross Road, the nearby **Borderline** or the **Rock Garden** in Covent Garden.

ANTELOPE PUBLIC HOUSE
210 Church Road
Leyton
London
E10 7BQ
Tel: 0208 539 3574
Mob: 07802 607663

The Antelope Public House is a traditional Irish pub. Entertainment includes traditional Irish music sessions at weekends. For your sporting enjoyment, all GAA games are televised on the pub's two big screens. Enjoy the friendly atmosphere and a great pint of Guinness.

THE BLARNEY STONE
89 Woodberry Grove
London
N4 2SB
Tel: 07930 386346
Mob: 0207 5033951

The Blarney Stone is a traditional Irish pub in the heart of North London. Named after the world-renowned Blarney Stone, this pub has friendly staff and good craic on offer all year round. Enjoy the atmosphere of a good crowd, especially when sporting events are televised on the pub's two big screens.

CHEVY CHASE
11 Leytonstone Road
Stratford
London
E15 1JA
Mob: 07980 874049

Chevy Chase, as seen on TG4, is a traditional Irish pub based in Stratford, London. Good craic is to be had at Irish music sessions Thursday, Friday and Saturday nights. For further entertainment, visitors can relax and enjoy all the sporting events on the pub's two big screens.

THE CHURCHILL ARMS
119 Kensignton Church Street
London W8 7LN
Tel: 0207 7274242

Named after Sir Winston Churchill, The Churchill Arms has welcomed the public for over 200 years. Boasting a traditional décor with wooden beams and two open fireplaces visitors can enjoy a Thai restaurant and a beautiful conservatory. Open 7 days from 11am-11pm. London Pub of the Year 1999.

EARL OF ESSEX
616 Romford Road
London
E12 5AF
Tel: 0208 533 5164
Mob: 07980 874049

The Earl of Essex is a traditional Irish pub situated on the main thoroughfare between Stratford and Ilford. Soon to be converted into a hotel with up to 17 en-suite rooms. All sports are televised on two big screens. Open until 2am at weekends. Visitors can enjoy traditional Irish music.

FILTHY MACNASTY'S WHISKEY CAFÉ
68 Amwell Street
London EC1
Tubes: Kings X/Angel/Farringdon
Tel: 0207 837 6067
Web: www.filthymacnastys.com

Filthy MacNasty's is a real pub for real people, selling the best Guinness in London as well as Czech Absinth, Irish Poteen and Honey Vodka. Second to none for character and atmosphere, Filthy's is the first stop for the international boozerati including Johnny Depp, Shane McGowan, Pete Libertine and many more.

FINBAR'S 225/225 Edgware Road Colindale, NW96LU Tel: 0208 9058853 Email: johnmcgowan@irishbars.demon.co.uk Web: www.irishbars.co.uk	This large bar offers traditional music and has large screens showing all sporting events. Large function room available and accommodation provided. Situated just minutes from Colindale Northern Line station. Enquire about management and staff positions.
FINBAR'S 330/336 Neasden Lane Neasden, NE 10 0AD Tel: 02084502220 Email: johnmcgowan@irishbars.demon.co.uk Web: www.irishbars.co.uk	Situated in the heart of Neasden Shopping Centre this venue is licensed until 5.00am with non-stop entertainment and good home-cooked food available. Function rooms available for all occasions as well as accommodation for long or short term. Enquire about management and staff positions.
FINBAR'S 88 Walm Lane Willesden Green, NW2 4QY Tel: 0208 830 1091 Email: johnmcgowan@irishbars.demon.co.uk Web: www.irishbars.co.uk	This fine traditional bar located opposite Willesden Green station offers entertainment nightly with function rooms available for all occasions and traditional meals served daily. Polite friendly staff and great craic. Visitors always welcome. Enquire about management and staff positions.
HAMMERS PUBLIC HOUSE 80 High St South Eastham London E6 6ET Tel: 0208 4721218 Mob: 07980 874049	This traditional East End pub enjoys a massive West Ham Football team following where you can enjoy the pub's two big screens in good company. A friendly atmosphere and a large beer garden create a welcoming setting for friends and families. Visit West Ham grounds only 1/4 mile from Hammers pub.
THE HARP 47 Chandos Place Trafalgar Square Charring Cross (opposite post office) Tel: 0208 4721218 Mob: 07980 874049	A friendly community boozer where the walls are covered with interesting oil paintings. It is a mildly bohemian little oasis in the middle of London that serves great English ales and sausages (featured in the good beer guide). Well worth a visit!

THE JAMES JOYCE
89/91 Kenton Road
Kenton
Harrow, HA3 0AN
Tel: 0208 9078791
Email:
johnmcgowan@irishbars.demon.co.uk
Web: www.irishbars.co.uk

Located next to Northwick Park station and open until midnight, this public house offers entertainment throughout the weekend and hosts various quiz nights. Plasma screens showing all sporting events. Home-cooked foods served. Enquire about management and staff positions.

PRINCESS OF WALES
25 Westham Lane
London
E15 4PH
Tel: 0208 519 2930
Mob: 07802 607663

The Princess of Wales is a family-run pub where food is served daily in a friendly and relaxing atmosphere. All major sporting events are televised live on the pub's two big screen TVs. Enjoy good food, good company and great live entertainment.

THE WELCOME INN
26/28 Cricklewood Lane
Cricklewood, NW2 1HB
Tel: 02084520608
Email:
johnmcgowan@irishbars.demon.co.uk
Web: www.irishbars.co.uk

Located just off the main Cricklewood Broadway and encompassing the spirit of old Ireland, this traditional house offers great entertainment daily and is open until midnight. Enquire about management and staff positions.

British restaurants now lead the world in the culinary arts. A new breed of super-chefs – as famous as the celebrity actors, artists and politicians who flock to their tables – are setting the standard for gourmets of haute cuisine everywhere. It is perhaps no coincidence that the best-selling cookbook in France, of all places, was written by British television chef Jamie Oliver. You will need to ring ahead to book a table at their restaurants but do be advised that the most popular evening and weekend times may be booked up a month or more in advance. Early evening or mid-week is often a safer bet.

Meals in these high-profile restaurants invariably produce high bills – if you want the best you have to pay for it and that means dinner starting at £50 per person. So take your credit card or plenty of cash. The biggest names include **La Gavroche**, on Upper Brook Street (French), **The Ivy**, on West Street (European), **Nobu**, on Old Park Lane (Japanese) and **Gordon Ramsay**'s restaurants, **Royal Hospital Road** and **Claridge's Hotel**, which are both haute cuisines. **Quaglino's**, on Bury Street (European), or the **River Café** (Italian), on Thames Wharf, are slightly less expensive.

Afternoon Tea and Scones are a tradition in London

British Cuisine

The best of British cooking can be found at **Fergus Henderson's** restaurant or **St John** in St John Street, Farringdon, where fresh seasonal produce reigns and there's a different fish dish every day. **Simpson's-in-the-Strand** is famous for its silver service traditional breakfasts, with devilled lamb kidneys, salmon and

lamb liver, kippers, Cumberland sausage and black pudding all on the menu. **Adam Street**, near Charing Cross, is a private club which is only open to the public at lunchtime. It does staple comfort food such as macaroni cheese, as well as standards like crispy pork belly and rhubarb crumble.

Leicester Square, a popular spot for cafés

Indian

Mahomet, a gentleman from Patna, Bihar, opened the first Indian restaurant, **The Hindostanee Coffee House,** in Portman Square in 1773. But it was only with large scale emigration from India, Pakistan, Sri Lanka, and Bangladesh especially, that the native Brits learned to love Indian food. There are 7,500 curry houses nationwide but, when it comes to sheer volume of restaurants in London, nothing can beat **Brick Lane** in the east of the city, where every second building seems to be a curry house. **Shampan** and **City Spice** offer authentic Bangladesh menus, while **Café Naz** is bright and breezy and offers a varied menu, including an excellent Dum-pukht (simmered) chicken biriani sealed in a break-covered pot. **The Sagar** on King Street, Hammersmith, specialises in the vegetarian cuisine of Karnataka, southern India, and is a favourite among curry fans. Each dish is a tasty fusion of vegetables and spices cooked in a wide variety of sauces.

Papageno

"Seeing is believing"

Nestling in the heart of London's bustling Covent Garden, Papageno is dedicated to pre and post-theatre dining.

Open all day, seven days a week; guests are invited to eat from an exclusive a la carte menu or choose from special set theatre meals available from £12.50.

A String Quartet performs every Sunday afternoon and Sunday & Monday evenings; and ad hoc appearances from a variety of artists take the venue centre stage.

Available for private functions, weddings, parties and other events for up to 700 guests, Papageno has one of London's most exquisite rooms with its own private entrance and bar.

29-31 Wellington Street, London. WC2
Tel: 020 7836 4444 Fax: 020 7836 0011
www.papagenorestaurant.com
Email: reservations@papagenorestaurant.com

Hays Galleria Market hosts a number of cafés and restaurants

Chinese

Chinese restaurants are as common in London as in any other city or small country town and the quality is quite often varied, sometimes simply catering for the characterless 'sweet and sour' end of the market. Of course there are great exceptions. The dim sum and main menu at Alan Yau's **Hakkasan** (Hanway Place) are good enough to have earned him a Michelin star, although a meal can be expensive. **Royal China** on Baker Street is cheaper but you may have to queue to get in. Dim sum here includes crab and asparagus dumplings and, more exotically, shark's fin. **Mr Chow** in Knightsbridge was established in 1968 and has remained popular since. The ambience and service are exemplary, the menu unusual and tasty, with duck and fish being specialities. A two-course set lunch is only £15.

Greek

London has a large Greek and Cypriot community thanks to old colonial links and most of the Greek restaurants are owned by expatriates. **Daphne**, on Bayham Street, Camden Town, has daily specials such as garídakia (prawns with feta in filo parcels) and on warm evenings you can sit out on its comfortable roof terrace. **Café Corfu**, also in Camden, specialises in dishes such as stuffed aubergines and crisped baby squid in a pastry basket. **The Real Greek**, in Hoxton Market, has fantastic mezédes (selections of hot and cold appetisers).

Other outstanding foreign menus include **Mandalay**, London's only Burmese restaurant. On Edgeware Road, this restaurant blends Chinese, Indian and Thai cooking with a Burmese twist and is great value for money. **Satay House** in Paddington serves genuine Malay dishes such as pungent fermented durian (not for those with a weak stomach), satay and spiced fish, all of which comes highly recommended. **Osia**, in the Haymarket, offers Australian delicacies such as kumera (sweet potato) and lemon myrtle with wattleseed cream. Some menu items are a bit expensive but there's a great buzz in the place. The **Churchill Thai Kitchen** in Kensington is very reasonable with main courses such as green chicken curry costing less than £6. It also has an alternative menu for non-Thai eaters.

Leadenhall Market

Quality Japanese food is widely available in London. Nobu leads the field, while **Matsuri** (High Holborn) and **Zuma** (Knightsbridge) are also notable eateries. **Pham Sushi** (Whitecross Street) serves fantastic sushi, sashimi, rice and noodles. It is unlicensed, so bring your own wine or beer.

American food isn't as well represented in London as you might expect, but **Belushi's** in Covent Garden is a great place to go for such cuisine, as is **Coyote Café** in Chiswick, where wild boar and zebra steak are on the menu. Ideally situated between Piccadilly and Leicester Square, **Planet Hollywood**, with its stunning décor and movie memorabilia, has a late night bar open until 3am and is the perfect venue for entertaining.

For more English-themed nosh, check out the **Elizabethan Banquet** in **Ivory House**, just yards from the Tower of London. This great family night out in London is a real step back in time.

Fish and chips are the other British national dish after curry and are usually bought from takeaway chip shops. But you can experience the peculiar delights of fried battered cod or haddock with large and crunchy chips at the **North Sea Fish Restaurant** in Leigh Street, behind the British Museum, where healthy eating is also catered for, or check out the **Rock & Sole Plaice** (great pun!), situated in Covent Garden.

Still in Covent Garden but more up-market, Richard Niazi's **Sarastro** restaurant is ideally located for opera- or theatre-goers. Guaranteeing great food in a lively atmosphere it has proved a popular choice since its opening. This success is repeated in its sister-venture **Papageno**, located on Wellington Street, just off Covent Garden. Conjuring a Middle-Eastern vibe and resplendent in its plush décor, Papageno promises a memorable eating experience and enjoyable night out.

Gastropubs

Over the past fourteen years numerous pubs in London have reinvented

Public parks are popular picnic locations when the weather is good

themselves as gastropubs, serving cheap, unfussy regional cuisine with a British flavour. The gastropub is really a British version of the French brasserie and the ones listed here are among the best.

The Eagle on Farringdon Road is the original and still the best gastropub and was established by Mike Belben and David Eyre in 1990. It offers a Mediterranean menu that changes twice daily. Oysters and sausages are one of the specialities to be found at **The Cow** in Westbourne Park Road, Notting Hill. The seafood platter is staggeringly big but there's roast chicken with girolles or entrecôte steak if you prefer to steer clear of shrimps, cockle, winkles and the other delights. Fashion designer Stella McCartney is a regular, apparently. On the same road is **The Oak**, where wafer-thin Neapolitan pizzas cooked in a wood-burning stove are the staple of a menu that also offers up loin of rabbit.

The seafood and fish theme continues a couple of kilometres away in **The Brackenbury** on Brackenbury Road, where seared scallops with guacamole and pan-fried sea bass with samphire bring in the customers which include a number of BBC television personalities.

Serving up British fare with a continental twist, **The Lansdowne** on Primrose Hill is another of the modern and stylish gastropubs worth checking out.

Eggs Benedict dripping in homemade hollandaise sauce, chicken and leek pie or salmon and smoked haddock fishcake are all on the enticing lunch menu in the **Builder's Arms** on Britten Street in Chelsea, while way across to the northwest of the city, **The House** (Canonbury Road, Islington) offers haddock velouté with poached egg. Its chef has a Michelin star to his name and the rich crab and scallop sausages in shellfish bisque shows why. One of the very best.

If you're on the tourist trail round the City, try the **Golden Heart** pub on Commercial Street, **La Grand Marque** wine bar on Ludgate Hill, or any of the cafés and restaurants in Leadenhall Market. If you're using the Gatwick Express flying in or out to Gatwick Airport, **Caffè Ritaz** is good for coffee at Victoria Station, where there is any number of stalls selling pretzels, muffins or sandwiches.

LISTINGS

THE LANSDOWNE PUB
90 Gloucester Avenue
Primrose Hill
NW1 8HX
Tel: 020 7483 0409
Tube: Chalk Farm
BR: Kentish Town

Pioneers in the gastro pub trade. The Lansdowne is a no-nonsense, fine-dining eaterie, committed to delivering top-notch Mediterranean-influenced food in a comfortable and friendly environment. A must-visit destination for any serious food fanatic.

THE MEDIEVAL BANQUET
Ivory House
St Katherine's Dock
London, E1W 1BP
UK
Tel: 020 7480 5353
Web: www.medievalbanquet.com

Join King Henry VIII and his special guests for a show of festive pageantry in the vaulted cellars of Ivory House, just a 'stones throw' from the Tower of London. Enjoy a four-course banquet with unlimited beer and wine followed by music and dancing until late.

Chelsea & Arsenal, London Soccer Derby

Sport is an obsession in London, with gyms, sports halls, stadiums and playing fields of every sort scattered around the city. But it is the professional sports that dominate the conversation in the capital's pubs, most of which will also show even minor games on television. The most popular sport is **football** (soccer), where the 'English disease' of crowd violence at matches is now largely a thing of the past, especially at the top level Premiership grounds.

Football

There are fourteen first-class football clubs in Greater London, as well as many more professional and semi-professional clubs in lower leagues. The five Premiership clubs are **Arsenal, Charlton, Chelsea, Fulham** and **Tottenham Hotspur** ('Spurs'). Tickets can be bought from the clubs or from agencies such as Ticketmaster but are expensive by European standards. Although big matches are usually sold out weeks in advance, tickets can often be obtained from touts either through newspaper advertisements or near the stadium on the day of the game. The standard of football at lower divisions clubs such as **Queens Park Rangers** or **Crystal Palace** is high and a visit there is always cheaper and often more enjoyable. You can usually pay on the day at these smaller clubs.

Most clubs are named after the area where they are based and can easily be reached by tube, urban railway or bus – Arsenal is the only club to have a tube station named after them (on the Piccadilly northern line). **Wembley**, the most famous stadium in the world, where England won the World Cup Final in 1966, is now being rebuilt, although without its famous towers.

Rugby

The magnificent stadium at **Twickenham** is home to English rugby, hosting internationals ('tests') and important cup matches. Tickets for internationals are almost unobtainable unless you are prepared to pay the extortionate prices asked by touts.

London's professional clubs playing Premiership rugby include: **Wasps**, **Saracens** and **London Irish**. While Saracens share a ground with **Watford Football Club**, historically, both London Irish and Wasps are London-based clubs but these days play outside the city; London Irish at the **Madejski Stadium** in Reading and Wasps at the **Wycombe Wanderers Football Club** ground in High Wycombe. There are many other semi-professional and amateur clubs all around Greater London, and all provide a matching level of competition between the teams and fervour amongst the fans. Matches are usually played on Saturday afternoons.

Cricket

Cricket, the national summer sport, is the most intellectual of team games. The complex rules and tactics make cricket an acquired taste but, although most games last from three to five days, the one-day version is more exciting and easier to understand. **Lord's Cricket Ground** is the sport's spiritual home.

Opened by pub owner Thomas Lord in St. John's Wood in 1814, Lord's is one of the most atmospheric international sports venues anywhere. Lord's and **The Oval**, on the south bank of the River Thames in Kennington, are where England play test matches every summer against teams from other Commonwealth countries such as Australia, India and South Africa. Both grounds are also home to county teams – Middlesex and Surrey, respectively – which play in the English professional league. Tickets for tests, which can last up to five days, are sold out months in advance but it is easier to get in to one-day internationals and county league games.

Tennis

There are many public and privately-run courts in Greater London but it is the leafy suburb of **Wimbledon** that is synonymous with tennis. Since 1877, the **All England Lawn Tennis and Croquet Club** has hosted the British championships, where past champions include John McEnroe, Pat Cash and Martina Navratilova. Wimbledon is a big part of the social season, as well known for the strawberries, cream and champagne consumed by spectators as for the thrilling lawn tennis. Spotting the celebrity is a popular pastime during breaks in play which, if the weather is unsettled, are frequent. Tickets for big games on the famous Centre Court are hard to get but, if you are prepared to queue, you can get in on the day to see stars like Roger Federer or Maria Sharpova playing on one of the many other courts in the complex. If you can't get in to see the tennis, enjoy a stroll on nearby **Wimbledon Common** and then take a drink in one of the area's many historic pubs.

Racing

Horse racing courses within easy travelling distance of London include **Ascot**, **Epsom**, **Windsor**, **Kempton** and **Sandown**. Racing is known as 'the sport of kings' and

Horse Racing

Ascot, in Berkshire, hosts an annual festival each June which is a brilliant blur of royalty, champagne and expensive attire. **The Derby**, the high spot of the racing calendar, is held in June on Epsom Downs in Surrey.

Greyhound racing takes places several times a week at Wimbledon and Walthamstow, in northeast London. There are also tracks slightly further out in Romford, Essex, and Dartford and Kent, which can be reached by train.

Athletics

There are two main athletics venues. Crystal Palace in southeast London hosts top-class international meetings featuring stars from the Olympics and World Championships each summer. The venerable **White City Stadium** in West London has witnessed many world records over the years. But the most impressive athletics event each year is a road race: the **London Marathon**, held each April, is the biggest sports event in the world in terms of both participants and spectators. More than 30,000 competitors – many in fancy dress and raising money for charity – complete the twenty-six mile course each year, starting at **Blackheath Park** and **Greenwich Park** in south London and then weaving their way into the city, cheered on by hundreds of thousands of spectators. The course loops around both banks of the River Thames, before finishing on the Mall alongside St. James's Park in Westminster.

London is a leading international centre for education and study. Every year, thousands of students arrive from other countries to study for qualifications at one of the city's many universities, colleges and schools.

Even though London is a multi-cultural city hosting many different nationalities and languages, the thing which binds its residents and visitors is the use of the English language, and many of London's students are there to improve their language skills.

There are many private schools which offer short, intensive courses for people wanting to learn English. They are busiest during the summer holidays (June-September). It is also possible for students to live in their teacher's home in order to benefit from intensive one-to-one teaching.

The advantages of learning English in London are manifold: there is a very wide choice of schools; students can live in the city centre in rooms or even in private homes; while studying, students get the chance to experience life in one of the world's great cities, enjoying shopping and cultural facilities rarely matched

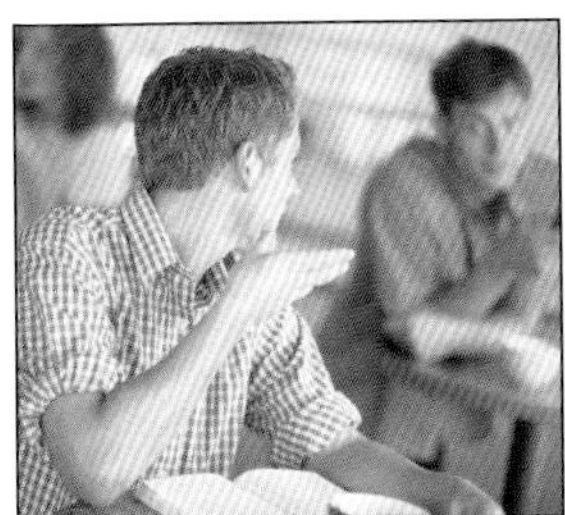

in Europe. And, if your English falters at first, you are almost certain to find someone who can speak your native tongue.

The well-established **Internexus London**, which is located at **Regent's College** in the heart of beautiful Regent's Park, is ideally located for experiencing life in London as well as for study, and it also provides a full accommodation service. Another centrally located education centre is **Aspect ILA** language school in **Holborn**. Housed in a listed building dating from the eighteenth century, this school is well equipped with a modern multimedia computer centre.

However, London's many language schools and their students are only one contemporary indication of the city's historic importance to the world of education and learning. London is also home to world-renowned universities such as **Imperial College** and the **London School of Economics**, where great thinkers have laid down many of the economic and political principles that guide the world today.

LISTINGS

ASPECT COLLEGE LONDON
3-4 Southampton Place
London, WC1A 2DA
Tel: +44(0) 20 7404 3080
Fax: +44(0) 20 7404 3443
Email: london@aspectworld.com
Web: www.aspectworld.com

Aspect College London, situated in the heart of Bloomsbury, specialises in University Preparation and General English Courses for international students. We also offer tailor-made group programmes and one-to-one tuition for executives. Accredited by the British Council.

INTERNEXUS LONDON
Regent's College
Inner Circle, Regent's Park
London NW1 4NS
England
Tel: 44 (0)20 7487 7489
Fax: 44 (0)20 7487 7409
Web: www.Internexus.to

Internexus is a small English Language school accredited by the British Council. We are part of the Regent's College Campus, in the centre of beautiful Regent's Park in central London. The college is surrounded by private gardens, sports fields, a boating lake and the famous Open Air Theatre.

You will find old buildings all over London which are part of this rich tradition of education and learning in England. The British Library on Euston Road, for instance, houses a treasure of books and documents which trace the development of the English language over the past 1,500 years. **Karl Marx** was a regular visitor to the old library when he was researching and writing his major political works.

For true fans of history and academia, no trip to the UK would be complete without a visit to one, or both, of the Oxbridge universities. **Oxford** and **Cambridge** are easily accessible from London. Trains leave from central London and private tour companies, such as Anderson Tours, can provide return coach travel.

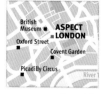

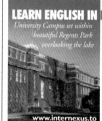

January
New Year's Day Parade, Central London

International Boat Show, Earls Court

Chinese New Year Celebrations, Soho

February
London Fashion Week, various venues

Accession Day Gun Salutes, Hyde Park & Tower of London

March
London Book Fair, ExCel Exhibition Centre

Oxford and Cambridge Boat Race, River Thames

Classic Motor Show, Alexandra Palace, Wood Green

April
London Marathon, Greenwich Park to The Mall

London Garden Show, Alexandra Palace, Wood Green

May
Royal Windsor Horse Show, Windsor

Chelsea Flower Show, Chelsea

London Dollhouse Festival, Kensington

June
Stella Artois Tennis Tournament, Queen's Club, Kensington

Trooping of the Colour, Whitehall

Wimbledon Lawn Tennis Championship, Wimbledon

July
British Beer Festival, London Olympia

Party in the Park, Hyde Park

The Proms, Royal Albert Hall

August
River Cultures Festival, River Thames

Notting Hill Carnival, Notting Hill

September
Brick Lane Festival, Brick Lane

Chelsea Antiques Fair, Chelsea

Covent Garden Festival of Street Theatre, Covent Garden

Mayor's Thames Festival, South Bank Centre

October
The Times London Film Festival, various venues

Trafalgar Square Festival, Trafalgar Square

November
Guy Fawkes Night celebration, throughout London

Lord Mayor's Procession and Show, Mansion House to Royal Courts of Justice

December
Olympia Show-jumping, London Olympia

Tower Bridge

ENGLISH	FRENCH	GERMAN	SPANISH	ITALIAN
GREETING & PHRASES				
hello	bonjour	hallo	hola	ciao
how are you?	comment allez vous?	Wie geht es Ihnen	¿como estás	come stai?
goodbye	au revoir	auf wiedersehen	adiós	arrivederci
I like	j'aime	ich möchte	me gusta	mi piace
thank you	merci	danke	gracias	grazie
please	s'il vous plaît	bitte	per favor	per favore
DIRECTIONS				
behind	derrière	hinten	detrás	dietro
beside	à côté de	neben	al lado	accanto
help	l'aide	die Hilfe	ayuda	aiuto
in front	devant	vor	en frente	davanti a
left	à gauche	links	izquierda	a sinistra
lost?	perdu	verloren	perdido	perduto
right	à droite	rechts	derecha	destra
straight ahead	tout a droit	immer geradeaus	todo recto	diritto
telephone	le téléphone	das Telefon	teléfono	telefono
ticket	le billet	die Karte	billete	biglietto
tourist office	le syndicat d'initiative	die Touristeninformation	información turística	ufficio turistico
turn	tournez	abbiegen (as in 'to turn left')	girar	girare
SITES				
castle	le château	das Schloss	castillo	castello
cathedral	la cathédrale	der Dom	catedral	cattedrale
church	l'église	die Kirche	iglesia	chiesa
library	la bibliothèque	die Bibliothek	biblioteca	biblioteca
museum	le musée	das Museum	museo	museo
statue	la statue	die Statue	estatua	statue
tour	la visite	die Tour	visita	gita
tower	la tour	der Turm	torre	torre
SHOPS AND SERVICES				
bank	la banque	die Bank	banco	banca
newsagents	le tabac-journaux	der Kiosk / das Zeitschriftengeschäft	quisco	Tabacaio/Giornalaio
pharmacy	la pharmacie	die Apotheke	farmacia	farmacia
pub	le pub	die Kneipe	pub	pub
restaurant	le restaurant	das Restaurant	restaurante	ristorante
shopping centre		das Einkaufszentrum	centro comercial	centro commerciale
supermarket	le supermarché	der Supermarkt	supermercado	supermercato
EMERGENCY				
accident	l'accident	der Unfall	accidente	incidente
assault		der Überfall	asalto	assalto
doctor	le docteur	der Arzt	médico	dottore
hospital	l'hôpital	das Krankenhaus	hospital	ospedale
injury	la blessure	die Verletzung	herida	ferita
police	la police	die Polizei	policia	polizia
thief	le voleur	der Dieb	ladrón	ladro

ENGLISH	FRENCH	GERMAN	SPANISH	ITALIAN
EATING OUT				
beer	la bière	das Bier	cerveza	birra
bill	l'addition	die Rechnung	la cuenta	conto
bread	le pain	das Brot	pan	pane
butter	le buerre	die Butter	mantequilla	burro
chicken	le poulet	das Huhn / Hühnchen	pollo	pollo
coffee	le café	der Kaffee	café	caffé
dessert	la dessert	der Nachtisch	postre	dolce
fish	le poisson	der Fisch	pescado	pesce
food	la nouriture	das Essen	comida	cibo
fruit	le fruit	das Obst	fruta	frutta
meat	la viande	das Fleisch	carne	carne
menu	le menu	das Menü	menu	menu
milk	le lait	die Milch	leche	latte
sandwich	le sandwich	das Sandwich / das belegte Brötchen	bocadillo	pannino
snack	le snack	der Imbiss	aperitivo	sputino
soup	la soupe	die Suppe	sopa	minestra
tea	le thé	der Tee	té	té
tip	le pourboire	das Trinkgeld	propina	mancia
vegetables	les légumes	das Gemüse	verdura	verdure
water	l'eau	das Wasser	agua	acqua
NUMBERS/ TIME				
hour	l'heure	die Stunde	hora	ora
minute	la minute	die Minute	minuto	minuto
second	la seconde	die Sekunde	segundo	secondo
this afternoon	cet après midi	heute Nachmittag	esta tarde	questo pomeriggio
this morning	ce matin	heute Morgen	esta mañana	questa mattina
today	aujourd'hui	heute	hoy	oggi
tomorrow	demain	Morgen	mañana	domani
yesterday	hier	gestern	ayer	ieri
one	une	Eins	uno	uno
two	deux	Zwei	dos	due
three	trois	Drei	tres	tre
four	quatre	Vier	cuatro	quattro
five	cinq	Fünf	cinco	cinque
six	six	Sechs	seis	sei
seven	sept	Sieben	siete	sette
eight	huit	Acht	ocho	otto
nine	neuf	Neun	nueve	nove
ten	dix	Zehn	diez	dieci
DAYS OF THE WEEK				
Monday	lundi	Montag	lunes	lunedi
Tuesday	mardi	Dienstag	martes	martedí
Wednesday	mercredi	Mittwoch	miércoles	mercoledí
Thursday	jeudi	Donnerstag	jeuves	giovedí
Friday	vendredi	Freitag	viernes	venerdi
Saturday	samedi	Samstag	sábado	sabato
Sunday	dimanche	Sonntag	domingo	domenica

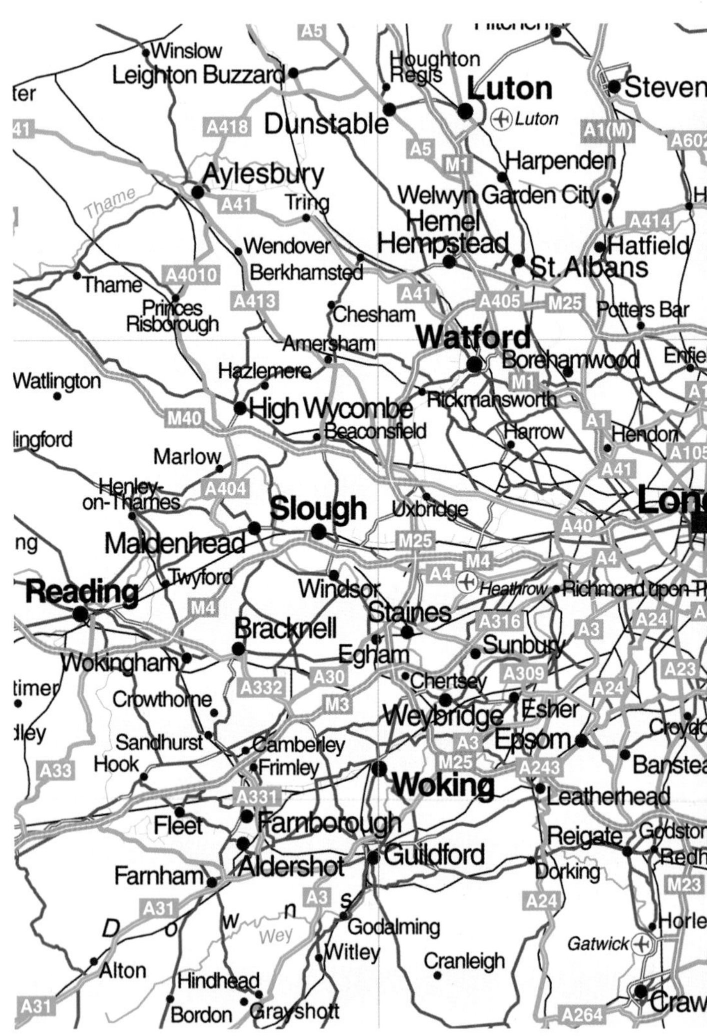

A5
Winslow
Leighton Buzzard
Houghton Regis
Luton
Dunstable
Luton
A1(M)
A418
A5
M1
Harpenden
Aylesbury
Thame
A41
Tring
Welwyn Garden City
Hemel Hempstead
A414
Wendover
Berkhamsted
Hatfield
St. Albans
Thame
A4010
Princes Risborough
A413
Chesham
A41
A405
M25
Potters Bar
Amersham
Watford
Borehamwood
Hazlemere
Watlington
M1
High Wycombe
Rickmansworth
M40
Beaconsfield
Harrow
A1
Hendon
Marlow
A41
Henley-on-Thames
A404
Slough
Uxbridge
A40
Maidenhead
M25
M4
A4
A4
Twyford
Heathrow
Richmond upon
Windsor
Reading
M4
Staines
A316
A24
Bracknell
A3
Egham
Sunbury
Wokingham
A30
A332
Chertsey
A309
A23
A24
Crowthorne
M3
Weybridge
Esher
Sandhurst
A3
Epsom
Camberley
A33
Hook
Frimley
M25
A243
Woking
A331
Leatherhead
Fleet
Farnborough
Reigate
Aldershot
Guildford
Farnham
Dorking
M23
A24
A3
A31
Wey
Godalming
Witley
Gatwick
Cranleigh
Alton
Hindhead
A31
Bordon
Grayshott
A264

Stansted Mountfitchet
Thaxted
Gosfield
West Bergholt
Braintree
Stansted
Great Dunmow
A120
Bishop's Stortford
Coggeshall
Kelvedon
A131
Sawbridgeworth
Witham
A12
Tiptree
Hertford
Harlow
A130
Tollesbury
M11
Chelmsford
Chelmer
Hoddesdon
A10
Chipping Ongar
A414
Maldon
Great Baddow
Cheshunt
Ingatestone
South Woodham Ferrers
A12
Billericay
Loughton
Wickford
M11
Rayleigh
Brentwood
A406
Redbridge
Romford
Rochford
Basildon
A12
South Benfleet
M25
A13
Southend
A13
Canvey Island
London City
Stanford le Hope
A102
Grays
Isle of Grain
A2
Tilbury
Wallend
Sheerness
Dartford
Gravesend
A2
A20
Gillingham
Isle of Sheppey
Swanley
A2
Bromley
Rochester
Chatham
Orpington
A232
Sittingbourne
New Addington
M20
A249
Aylesford
M2
M26
Caterham
A25
A228
M25
Sevenoaks
Maidstone
Oxted
A21
A26
A229
M20
A22
Tonbridge
Headcorn
Lingfield
Edenbridge
Paddock Wood
Staplehurst
Southbridge
Pembury
Biddenden
East Grinstead
Royal Tunbridge Wells
Forest Row
A21

Chesham
Chalfont & Latimer
Watford
Amersham
Chorleywood
Croxley
Rickmansworth
Moor Park
Northwood
Northwood Hills
Pinner
North Harrow
Harrow-on-the-Hill
West Ruislip
Hillingdon
Ruislip
Ruislip Manor
Uxbridge
Ickenham
Eastcote
Ruislip Gardens
Rayners Lane
West Harrow
South Ruislip
Northolt
Greenford
South Harrow
Sudbury Hill
Sudbury Town
Alperton
Perivale
Hanger Lane
Park Royal
North Ealing
Ealing Broadway
Ealing Common
South Ealing
Northfields
Boston Manor
Hounslow East
Osterley
Hounslow West
Hounslow Central
Heathrow Terminals 1, 2, 3
Hatton Cross
for Heathrow Terminal 4
Bus service
Heathrow Terminal 4
Heathrow Terminal 4 Underground station closed from 7 January 2005 - September 2006. Replacement bus services run from Hatton Cross.
Harrow & Wealdstone
Kenton
Northwick Park
Preston Road
South Kenton
North Wembley
Wembley Central
Wembley Park
Stonebridge Park
Harlesden
Willesden Junction
Kensal Green
Queen's Park
Kilburn Park
Maida Vale
Warwick Avenue
Paddington
Royal Oak
Westbourne Park
Ladbroke Grove
Latimer Road
North Acton
West Acton
East Acton
White City
Acton Central
South Acton
Acton Town
Chiswick Park
Turnham Green
Stamford Brook
Ravenscourt Park
Gunnersbury
Kew Gardens
Richmond
Shepherd's Bush
Goldhawk Road
Hammersmith
Barons Court
West Kensington
Kensington (Olympia)
Earl's Court
West Brompton
Fulham Broadway
Parsons Green
Putney Bridge
East Putney
Southfields
Wimbledon Park
Wimbledon
River Thames
Stanmore
Canons Park
Queensbury
Kingsbury
Neasden
Dollis Hill
Willesden Green
Kilburn
Brondesbury Park
Kensal Rise
Brondesbury
West Hampstead
Finchley Road
Swiss Cottage
St. John's Wood
Finchley Road & Frognal
Edgware
Burnt Oak
Colindale
Hendon Central
Brent Cross
Golders Green
Hampstead
Hampstead Heath
Belsize Park
Chalk Farm
Camden Town
Mornington Crescent
Great Portland Street
Euston
Baker Street
Edgware Road
Marylebone
Warren Street
Bayswater
Regent's Park
Holland Park
Queensway
Lancaster Gate
Bond Street
Oxford Circus
Notting Hill Gate
Marble Arch
Tottenham Court Road
High Street Kensington
Hyde Park Corner
Green Park
Piccadilly Circus
Knightsbridge
Gloucester Road
South Kensington
Sloane Square
St. James's Park
Victoria
Westminster
Waterloo
Pimlico
Vauxhall
Stockwell
Oval
Clapham North
Clapham High Street
Clapham Common
Clapham South
Balham
Tooting Bec
Tooting Broadway
Colliers Wood
South Wimbledon
Morden
Bakerloo
Central
Circle
District
East London
Hammersmith & City
Jubilee
Metropolitan
Northern
Piccadilly
Victoria
Waterloo & City
DLR
Under construction
National Rail
© Transport for London